SUPER SEATWORK

Word Skills

Mary Pecci
440 Davis Ct. #405
San Francisco, CA 94111

Copyright © 1980 Mary F. Pecci

All Rights Reserved

Permission is granted to reproduce
this material for classroom use.

Last Printing 1991

Distributed by:

PECCI EDUCATIONAL PUBLISHERS
440 Davis Court, No. 405
San Francisco, CA 94111

ISBN NO. 0-943220-04-1

These materials are derived from:
AT LAST! A READING METHOD FOR EVERY CHILD!
Written by: Mary F. Pecci, Reading Specialist
Edited by: Ernest F. Pecci, Child Psychiatrist

Acknowledgements

I would like to extend my sincere appreciation to the following teachers for their valuable suggestions and contributions and for allowing me to test these materials in their classrooms: Patricia Armanini, Marilynne Bachli, Pat Barrett, Dorothy Brus, Leonarda Brush, Lori Davis, Manota Lyons, Laurel Manders, and June Triesch - with a special thanks to my irreplaceable aides, Marilyn Siacotos and Marilynn Mager.

To my friends and relatives, Norma Gallant, Maria Abregana, my sister Dorene Pecci Nocera, nephews Mark Kelley and Johnny Pecci, nieces Kristine Kelley, Caroline Kelley, and Diana Pecci (for providing the jokes), and to Dick Turner, Jack Emmetts, and Dick Heather of Copy Control Systems One Embarcadero Center, San Francisco, for their invaluable assistance.

And to my wonderful pupils over the past 18 years, who have guided the direction of this work.

For comprehensive details on how to teach reading, order AT LAST! A READING METHOD FOR EVERY CHILD! This book presents a simple phonic technique which eliminates all of the nitty-gritty and tedium which causes failure. It was developed during 10 years of research and has proven successful with every possible type of reading disability - at Juvenile Court, in the ghettos, with all socio-economic groups, with the mentally retarded, English second language students and those who have been professionally diagnosed as having learning disability, neurological handicaps and dyslexia. Also included is a multitude of motivation and reinforcement techniques which have been collected over the years from master teachers.

Other books by Mary Pecci:

SUPER SEATWORK - Content Areas

SUPER SEATWORK - Letter Recognition

SUPER SEATWORK - Linguistic Exercises

SUPER SEATWORK - Color Words

SUPER SEATWORK - Number Words

SUPER SEATWORK - Phonic Grab Bag

How to Discipline Your Class For Joyful Teaching!

Introduction

Here under one cover, so you won't have to search high and low, is everything you need to teach the basic word skills that are inseparable from reading instruction and which pave the way toward independent reading.

Written in developmental levels of vocabulary, with one clear message on a page, these exercises make for easy teaching and learning - allowing average students to progress at a comfortable pace, gifted students to proceed at their own pace, while providing a means for accelerating below-level students.

For maximum effectiveness, do each assignment with the students, guiding participation at each step, before assigning it for independent seatwork. In this way, they will have a clear understanding of the skill to be learned and the procedure for completing the exercise.

Borne in the classroom, tempered by trial and error, child-proofed by student feedback, these exercises provide a proper balance of format, repetition, and variety to produce mastery at each step.

CONTENTS

Page

I. Roots and Endings:

Add:
- s — 1-2
- es — 3-4
- ed — 5-6
- d — 7-8
- ing — 9-10
- REVIEW — 11-12
- Change it Back! — 13

Add:
- er — 14
- er, est — 15-16
- r — 17
- r, st — 18
- REVIEW — 19

Add:
- en — 20
- n — 21
- Change it Back! — 22

Add:
- y — 23
- ly — 24-25
- ful — 26-27
- Change it Back! — 28

Drop e and add ing — 29-31
- Change it Back! — 32-33

Change y to i and add es — 34-36
Change y to i and add ed — 37
Change y to i and add es — 38

	Page
Change y to i and add ed	39
REVIEW	40-41
Change it Back!	42
Change y to i and add er, est	43-44
Change y to i and add ly, ness	45
Change y to i and add eth, ous	46
Change it Back!	47-48
Add s after ey	49
Change f to v and add es	50-51
Change it Back!	52
Double the consonant to keep the vowel short and add:	
ed	53
ing	54
er, ing	55
er, est	56
Change it Back!	57
II COMPOUND WORDS	58-68
III POSSESSIVES	69-79
IV CONTRACTIONS:	
not	80-82
will, have, has	83-86
is	87-89
am, are, us, would	90-93
REVIEW	94-95

	Page
V PREFIXES:	
un, en	96
re, de	97
REVIEW	98
mis, dis	99
in, im	100
REVIEW	101
pre-sub	102
bi-semi	103
mid, fore, non, anti	104
REVIEW	105-106
VI SUFFIXES:	
(All word endings are suffixes. However, they are usually referred to as suffixes only after the children have progressed from the basic vocabulary to multisyllabic words.)	
less, ness	107
ish, able	108
REVIEW	109
ward, ment	110
ship, hood	111
REVIEW	112
ant, ist, age	113
some, ous, ance	114
REVIEW	115
Double Suffixes:	
fully, fulness	116
ishness, ening, ingly	117
REVIEW	118
VII PREFIXES and SUFFIXES	119-121

VIII SYLLABLES:

(The following 8 reliable rules will give the students the ability to handle syllables for all practical purposes. Many times, too many rules, exceptions, and complicated formulas do more to confuse than help - especially in cases where the rule is only as good as its number of exceptions. Those rules are really unnecessary anyway because words are divided into syllables in the dictionary.)

	Page
Introduction to Syllables	122-124
Accent Marks	125-127

Rules:
1. Divide between the double consonant.	128-129
2. Divide between the unlike consonants.	130-131
3. The consonant joins the _le_.	132-133
4. Divide between the root and ending.	134-135
5. Divide between compound words.	136-137
REVIEW	138-144
6. Don't split a Digraph or Blend.	145-146
7. Divide after the long vowel.	147-148
8. One vowel can be a syllable.	149-150
REVIEW	151-157

IX DICTIONARY SKILLS:

Dictionary Diagram	158

Alphabetizing:
Alphabet Sequence	159-169
Use the first letter to alphabetize.	170-174
Use the second letter to alphabetize.	175
Use the third letter to alphabetize.	176
Use the fourth letter to alphabetize.	177
Use the fifth letter to alphabetize.	178
Use the sixth letter to alphabetize.	179
REVIEW	180-182

	Page
Entry Words	183-184
Dividing the Dictionary	185-187
Guide Words	188-194
Word Definitions	195-199
Multiple Meanings	200-201

The Pronunciation Key:

Introduction	202-204

Going Thru the Key:

Long and Short Vowel Symbols	205
REVIEW	206
Let's Write It!	207-211
Consonant Symbols:	
c=k, c=s, g=j	212
x=ks, q=kw	213
REVIEW	214
Other Vowel Symbols	215
Let's Write It!	216-219
Other Consonant Symbols:	
th and t̶h̶	220
REVIEW	221-223
The Schwa (ə) Symbol	224-226
REVIEW	227
The zh Symbol	228
Let's Write It!	229
REVIEW	230-233
– Answer Key –	234-238

Name: _____

ROOTS and ENDINGS
Add S

Directions: (1) Read each word. (2) Write each word with the ending "s." (3) Read the new word you wrote. (4) Reread the completed paper going across.

Name: _____

ROOTS and ENDINGS
Add S

<u>Directions</u>: (1) Read each word. (2) Write each word with the ending "s." (3) Read the new word you wrote. (4) Reread the completed paper going across.

1. get
2. come
3. see
4. want
5. ride
6. stop
7. take
8. find

Name: _____

ROOTS and ENDINGS
Add es

Directions: (1) Read each word. (2) Write each word with the ending "es." (3) Read the new word you wrote. (4) Reread the completed paper going across.

 dress  _____

 box  _____

 bus   _____

 glass   _____

 church   _____

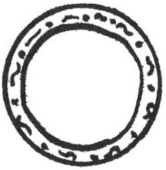 dish  _____

Name: _____

Roots and ENDINGS
Add es

Directions: (1) Read each word. (2) Write each word with the ending "es." (3) Read the new word you wrote. (4) Read the completed paper going across.

1. wish
2. cross
3. march
4. push
5. kiss
6. dash
7. flash
8. rush

Name:

ROOTS and ENDINGS
Add ed

Directions: (1) Read each word. (2) Write each word with the ending "ed." (3) Read the new word you wrote. (4) Reread the completed paper going across.

1. want
2. need
3. start
4. end
5. wait
6. plant
7. lift
8. land

Name:

ROOTS and ENDINGS
Add ed

play
played

Directions: (1) Read each word. (2) Write each word with the ending "ed." (3) Read the new word you wrote. (4) Reread the completed paper going across.

1. play
2. jump
3. help
4. look
5. work
6. call
7. walk
8. ask

Name:

ROOTS and ENDINGS

If the word ends in e, add just d.

Directions: (1) Read each word. (2) Write each word with the ending "d." (3) Read the new word you wrote. (4) Reread the completed paper going across.

1. like
2. bake
3. hope
4. tame
5. hike
6. rake
7. joke
8. smile

Name:

Roots and Endings
If the word ends in e, add just d.

Directions: (1) Read each word. (2) Write each word with the ending "d." (3) Read the new word you wrote. (4) Reread the completed paper going across.

1. save
2. pile
3. dare
4. time
5. poke
6. share
7. file
8. scare

Name:

ROOTS and ENDINGS
Add ing

Directions: (1) Read each word. (2) Write each word with the ending "ing." (3) Read the new word you wrote. (4) Reread the completed paper going across.

1. look
2. go
3. jump
4. help
5. want
6. play
7. see
8. do

10

Name:

ROOTS and ENDINGS
Add ing

<u>Directions</u>: (1) Read each word. (2) Write each word with the ending "ing." (3) Read the new word you wrote. (4) Reread the completed paper going across.

1. call

2. walk

3. ask

4. tell

5. say

6. be

7. end

8. fill

Name: _____

Roots and ENDINGS

Directions: (1) Read each word. (2) Write each word with the endings "s," "ed," and "ing." (3) Read the new words you wrote. (4) Reread the completed paper going across.

Root	Add s	Add ed	Add ing
1. want			
2. lift			
3. need			
4. start			
5. wait			
6. land			

Name: _____

Roots and ENDINGS

Directions: (1) Read each word. (2) Write each word with the endings "s," "ed," and "ing." (3) Read the new words you wrote. (4) Reread the completed paper going across.

Root	Add s	Add ed	Add ing
1. help			
2. look			
3. jump			
4. walk			
5. ask			
6. play			

Name:

Change it Back!

Directions: (1) Read each word. (2) Write just the root of the word. (3) Read the new word you wrote. (4) Reread the completed paper going across.

Root and Ending	Root Word
1. looking	
2. wanted	
3. boys	
4. liked	
5. dishes	
6. played	
7. jumping	
8. works	

14

Name: _____

ROOTS and ENDINGS
Add er

Directions: (1) Read each word. (2) Write each word with the ending "er." (3) Read the new word you wrote. (4) Read the completed paper going across.

1. work
2. farm
3. paint
4. jump
5. catch
6. sleep
7. fight
8. teach

Name: _____

Roots and ENDINGS

Directions: (1) Read each word. (2) Write each word with the endings "er" and "est". (3) Read the new words you wrote. (4) Reread the completed paper going across.

Root	Add er	Add est
1. fast		
2. tall		
3. quick		
4. neat		
5. loud		
6. cold		

Name: _____

ROOTS and ENDINGS

Directions: (1) Read each word. (2) Write each word with the endings "er" and "est". (3) Read the new word you wrote. (4) Reread the completed paper going across.

Root	Add er	Add est
1. long		
2. old		
3. soft		
4. clean		
5. deep		
6. small		

Name:

ROOTS and ENDINGS
If the word ends in e, add just r.

rider

Directions: (1) Read each word. (2) Write each word with the ending "r." (3) Read the new word you wrote. (4) Reread the completed paper going across.

1. ride

2. joke

3. skate

4. drive

5. move

6. race

7. dine

8. write

Name: _____

Roots and ENDINGS

Directions: (1) Read each word. (2) Write each word with the endings "r" and "st." (3) Read the new words you wrote. (4) Reread the completed paper going across.

Root	Add r	Add st
1. fine		
2. late		
3. brave		
4. wide		
5. ripe		
6. safe		

Name: _____

ROOTS and ENDINGS

Directions: (1) Read each word. (2) Write each word with the endings "s," "ed," "er," and "ing." (3) Read the new words you wrote. (4) Reread the completed paper going across.

Root	Add s	Add ed	Add er	Add ing
play				
jump				
call				
work				
paint				
farm				

Roots and ENDINGS
Add en

<u>Directions</u>: (1) Read each word. (2) Write each word with the ending "en." (3) Read the new word you wrote. (4) Reread the completed paper going across.

1. bright
2. sharp
3. weak
4. fright
5. sweet
6. quick
7. tight
8. hard

Name: _____

ROOTS and ENDINGS

If the word ends in e, add just n.

Directions: (1) Read each word. (Write each word with the ending "n." (3) Read the new word you wrote. (4) Reread the completed paper going across.

1. give
2. take
3. ripe
4. broke
5. like
6. shave
7. drive
8. froze

22

Name:

Change it Back!

Directions: (1) Read each word. (2) Write just the root of the word. (3) Read the new word you wrote. (4) Re-read the completed paper going across.

Root and Ending	Root Word
1. worker	
2. later	
3. helped	
4. safest	
5. given	
6. deeper	
7. sweeten	
8. calls	

Name:

ROOTS and ENDINGS
Y on the end says "ee."

Directions: (1) Read each word. (2) Write each word with the ending "y." (3) Read the new word you wrote. (4) Reread the completed paper going across.

1. luck
2. sleep
3. rock
4. wind
5. curl
6. rain
7. dust
8. hill

Name:

Roots and ENDINGS
Add ly

Directions: (1) Read each word. (2) Write each word with the ending "ly." (3) Read the new word you wrote. (4) Reread the completed paper going across.

1. friend
2. like
3. real
4. hard
5. nice
6. slow
7. glad
8. safe

Name:

ROOTS and ENDINGS
Add ly

Directions: (1) Read each word. (2) Write each word with the ending "ly." (3) Read the new word you wrote. (4) Reread the completed paper going across.

1. soft
2. quick
3. bold
4. bright
5. quiet
6. shy
7. wise
8. neat

Name:

ROOTS and ENDINGS
Add ful

Directions: (1) Read each word. (2) Write each word with the ending "ful." (3) Read the new word you wrote. (4) Reread the completed paper going across.

(helpful)

1. help
2. play
3. thank
4. hope
5. care
6. use
7. cheer
8. faith

Name: _____

ROOTS and ENDINGS
Add ful

Directions: (1) Read each word. (2) Write each word with the ending "ful." (3) Read the new word you wrote. (4) Reread the completed paper going across.

1. wish
2. color
3. forget
4. thought
5. rest
6. pain
7. wonder
8. truth

Name:

Change it Back!

Directions: (1) Read each word. (2) Write just the root of the word. (3) Read the new word you wrote. (4) Reread the completed paper going across.

Root and Ending	Root Word
1. lucky	
2. taken	
3. longest	
4. helpful	
5. taller	
6. softly	
7. weaken	
8. safer	

Name: _____

Roots and ENDINGS
Drop e and adding ing.

Directions: (1) Read each word. (2) Cross out the "e" and write "ing" above it. (3) Write this new word in the next column. (4) Read the new word you wrote. (5) Reread the completed paper.

1. com~~e~~ ^ing   coming
2. take
3. like
4. joke
5. ride
6. hope
7. give
8. have

29

Roots and Endings
Drop e and add ing.

Directions: (1) Read each word. (2) Cross out the "e" and write "ing" above it. (3) Write this new word in the next column. (4) Read the new word you wrote. (5) Reread the completed paper.

1. make
2. hide
3. smile
4. wipe
5. name
6. bite
7. save
8. dare

Name:

ROOTS and ENDINGS
Drop e and add ing.

use — using

Directions: (1) Read each word. (2) Cross out "e" and write "ing" above it. (3) Write this new word in the next column. (4) Read the new word you wrote. (5) Reread the completed paper.

1. use
2. bake
3. move
4. share
5. vote
6. write
7. pile
8. care

Name:

Change it Back!

Directions: (1) Read each word. (2) Write just the root of the word. (3) Read the new word you wrote. (4) Re-read the completed paper going across.

Roots and Endings	Root Word
1. riding	
2. coming	
3. smiling	
4. making	
5. hoping	
6. saving	
7. giving	
8. having	

Name: _____

Change it Back!

Directions: (1) Read each word. (2) Write just the root of the word. (3) Read the new word you wrote. (4) Reread the completed paper going across.

Root and Ending	Root Word
1. liking	
2. joking	
3. hiding	
4. saving	
5. writing	
6. naming	
7. using	
8. moving	

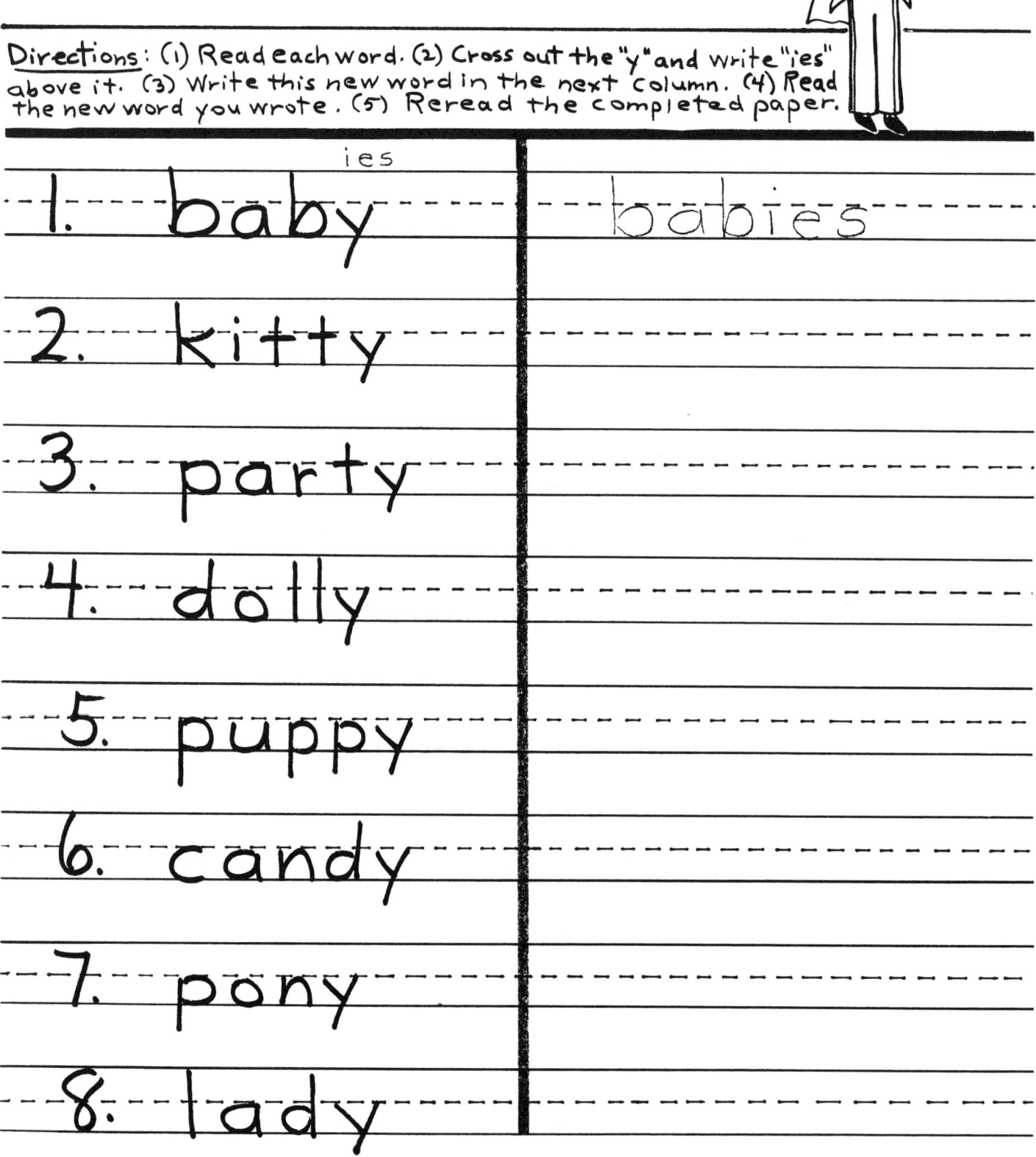

Name: _____

ROOTS and ENDINGS
Change y to i and add es.

Directions: (1) Read each word. (2) Cross out the "y" and write "ies" above it. (3) Write this new word in the next column. (4) Read the new word you wrote. (5) Reread the completed paper.

1. penny
2. story
3. cherry
4. city
5. bunny
6. sixty
7. hobby
8. family

Roots and Endings
change y to i and add es.

Directions: (1) Read each word. (2) Cross out the "y" and write "ies" above it. (3) Write this new word in the next column. (4) Read the new word you wrote. (5) Reread the completed paper.

carries

1. carry
2. study
3. copy
4. empty
5. worry
6. marry
7. hurry
8. bully

Name:

ROOTS and ENDINGS
change y to i and add ed.

Directions: (1) Read each word. (2) Cross out the "y" and write "ied" above it. (3) Write this new word in the next column. (4) Read the new word you wrote. (5) Reread the completed paper.

1. hurry
2. carry
3. study
4. copy
5. worry
6. empty
7. bully
8. marry

Name:

Roots and Endings
change y to i and add es.

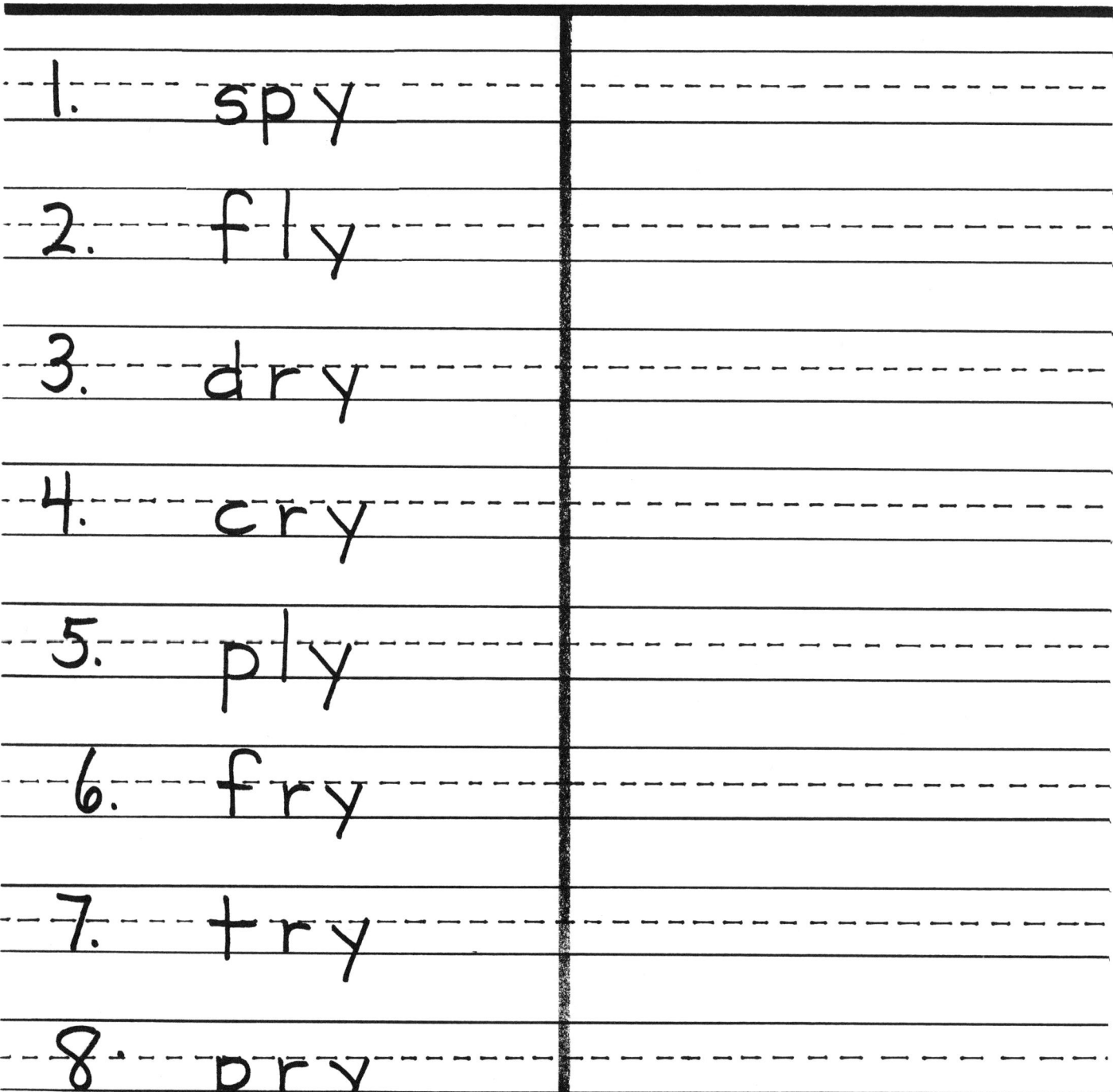

Directions: (1) Read each word. (2) Cross out the "y" and write "ies" above it. (3) Write this new word in the next column. (4) Read the new word you wrote. (5) Reread the completed paper.

1. spy
2. fly
3. dry
4. cry
5. ply
6. fry
7. try
8. pry

Name:

ROOTS and ENDINGS
change y to i and add ed.

Directions: (1) Read each word. (2) Cross out the "y" and write "ied" above it. (3) Write this new word in the next column. (4) Read the new word you wrote. (4) Reread the completed paper.

1. try
2. cry
3. fly
4. pry
5. spy
6. ply
7. dry
8. fry

Name: _____

Roots and Endings

Directions: (1) Read each word. (2) Write each word with the new endings. (3) Read the new words you wrote. (4) Reread the completed paper going across.

Root	Change y to i and add es.	Change y to i and added ed.
1. copy		
2. hurry		
3. study		
4. carry		
5. empty		
6. worry		

Name: _____

ROOTS and ENDINGS

Directions: (1) Read each word. (2) Write each word with the new endings. (3) Read the new words you wrote. (4) Reread the completed paper going across.

Root	Change y to i and add es.	Change y to i and add ed.
1. cry		
2. fry		
3. dry		
4. try		
5. spy		
6. fly		

Name: _____

Change it Back!

Directions: (1) Read each word. (2) Write just the root of the word. (3) Read the new word you wrote. (4) Reread the completed paper going across.

Root and Ending	Root Word
1. carries	
2. flies	
3. hurried	
4. cried	
5. copies	
6. dries	
7. studied	
8. tried	

Name: _____

Roots and ENDINGS

Directions: (1) Read each word. (2) Write each word with the new endings. (3) Read the new words you wrote. (4) Reread the completed paper going across.

Root	Change y to i and add er.	Change y to i and add est.
1. happy		
2. pretty		
3. busy		
4. early		
5. shiny		
6. easy		

happier

Name: _____

Roots and ENDINGS

Directions: (1) Read each word. (2) Write each word with the new endings. (3) Read the words you wrote. (4) Reread the completed paper going across.

Root	Change y to i and add er.	Change y to i and add est.
1. friendly		
2. lucky		
3. sleepy		
4. hungry		
5. lazy		
6. sunny		

Name: _____

ROOTS and ENDINGS
change y to i and add ly.

Directions: (1) Read each word. (2) Cross out the "y" and write "ily" over it. (3) Write this new word in the next column. (4) Read the new word you wrote.

1. happy	
2. easy	
3. busy	
4. sleepy	

change y to i and add ness.

Directions: (1) Read each word. (2) Cross out the "y" and write "iness" above it. (3) Write this new word in the next column. (4) Read the new word you wrote. (5) Reread the completed paper.

1. happy	
2. easy	
3. busy	
4. sleepy	

45

Name:
ROOTS and ENDINGS
Change y to i and add eth.

twentieth

Directions: (1) Read each word. (2) Cross out "y" and write "ieth" above it. (3) Write this new word in the next column. (4) Read the new word you wrote.

1. twenty
2. thirty
3. forty
4. fifty

Change y to i and add ous.

Directions: (1) Read each word. (2) Cross out "y" and write "ious" above it. (3) Write this new word in the next column. (4) Read the new word you wrote. (4) Reread the completed paper.

1. glory
2. mystery
3. victory
4. injury

Name:

Change it Back!

Directions: (1) Read each word. (2) Write just the root of the word. (3) Read the new word you wrote. (4) Reread the completed paper going across.

Root and Ending	Root Word
1. tries	
2. luckier	
3. families	
4. happiest	
5. studied	
6. laziest	
7. cities	
8. shinier	

Name: _____

Change it Back!

Directions: (1) Read each word. (2) Write just the root of the word. (3) Read the new word you wrote. (4) Reread the completed paper going across.

Root and ENDING	Root Word
1. easily	
2. twentieth	
3. happily	
4. glorious	
5. sleepiness	
6. fiftieth	
7. easiness	
8. victorious	

Name:

ROOTS and ENDINGS
If the word ends in ey, add just s.

Directions: (1) Read each word. (2) Write each word with the ending "s." (3) Read the new word you wrote. (4) Reread the completed paper going across.

 monkey  _____

 trolley   _____

 turkey   _____

 chimney  _____

 donkey  _____

 key  _____

Name: _____

ROOTS and ENDINGS
Change f to v and add es.

Directions: (1) Read each word. (2) Cross out the "f" and write "ves" above it. (3) Write this new word in the next column. (4) Read the new word you wrote. (5) Reread the completed paper.

1. leaf
2. wife
3. loaf
4. elf
5. half
6. life
7. calf
8. thief

Name: _____

ROOTS and ENDINGS

Change f to v and add es.

Directions: (1) Read each word. (2) Cross out the "f" and write "ves" over it. (3) Write this new word in the next column. (4) Read the new word you wrote. (5) Reread the completed paper.

1. scarf
2. wolf
3. knife
4. dwarf
5. shelf
6. wharf
7. self

Note: "Scarf," "dwarf," and "wharf" also form their plurals by adding just s.

Name: _____

Change it Back!

Directions: (1) Read each word. (2) Write just the root of the word. (3) Read the new word you wrote. (4) Reread the completed paper going across.

Root and Ending	Root Word
1. wives	
2. shelves	
3. halves	
4. lives	
5. thieves	
6. leaves	
7. knives	
8. elves	

ROOTS and ENDINGS

Double the consonant to keep the vowel short.

<u>Directions:</u> (1) Read each word. (2) Write each word with a double final consonant and add "ed." (3) Read the new word you wrote. (4) Reread the completed paper.

1. stop
2. hug
3. wag
4. hop
5. drop
6. trip
7. shop
8. rub

54

Name: _____

ROOTS and ENDINGS

Double the consonant to keep the vowel short.

Directions: (1) Read each word. (2) Write each word with a double final consonant and add "ing." (3) Read the new word you wrote. (4) Reread the completed paper.

1. run
2. get
3. tag
4. put
5. nap
6. sit
7. rip
8. swim

Name: _____

ROOTS and ENDINGS

Directions: (1) Read each word. (2) Write each word with the new endings. (3) Read the new words you wrote. (4) Reread the completed paper.

Root	Double the consonant and add **er**.	Double the consonant and add **ing**.
1. hit		
2. run		
3. swim		
4. plan		
5. quit		
6. win		

Name: _____

Roots and ENDINGS

<u>Directions</u>: (1) Read each word. (2) Write each word with the new endings. (3) Read the new words you wrote. (4) Reread the completed paper.

Root	Double the consonant and add <u>er</u>.	Double the consonant and add <u>est</u>.
1. big		
2. wet		
3. hot		
4. sad		
5. dim		
6. red		

Name: _____

Change it Back!

Mager the Magician

Directions: (1) Read each word. (2) Write just the root of the word. (3) Read the new word you wrote. (4) Reread the completed paper.

Root and Ending	Root Word
1. getting	
2. stopped	
3. winner	
4. biggest	
5. wagging	
6. wetter	
7. hottest	
8. swimmer	

58

Name: _____

COMPOUND WORDS

When two words are put together to form one word, it is called a compound word.

Directions: (1) Draw a connecting line from each two words on the left to the corresponding compound word on the right.

in to   without

to day   someone

with out   into

some one   today

Directions: (1) Read each compound word. (2) Divide each compound word and write the two separate words. (3) Reread the completed paper going across.

1. without = with out

2. someone = _____

3. into = _____

4. today = _____

Name:

COMPOUND WORDS

When two words are put together to form one word, it is called a compound word.

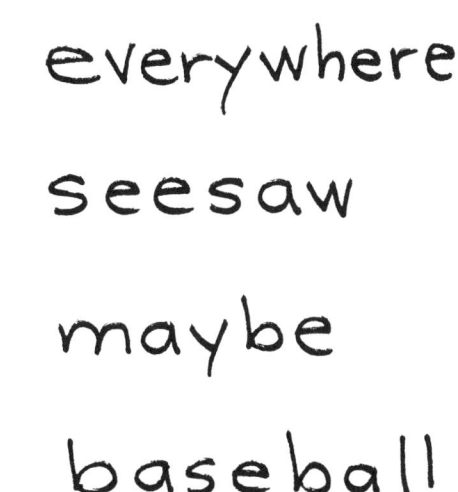

Directions: (1) Draw a connecting line from each two words on the left to the corresponding compound word on the right.

see saw   everywhere

may be   seesaw

base ball   maybe

every where   baseball

Directions: (1) Read each compound word. (2) Divide each compound word and write the two separate words. (3) Reread the completed paper going across.

1. maybe   = _____

2. everywhere = _____

3. baseball   = _____

4. seesaw   = _____

Name: _____

COMPOUND WORDS

When two words are put together to form one word, it is called a compound word.

Directions: (1) Draw a connecting line from each two words on the left to the corresponding compound word on the right.

under stand   beside

every one   everyone

home work   homework

be side   understand

Directions: (1) Read each compound word. (2) Divide each compound word and write the two separate words. (3) Reread the completed paper going across.

1. beside   = _____

2. homework   = _____

3. everyone   = _____

4. understand = _____

COMPOUND WORDS

When two words are put together to form one word, it is called a compound word.

Directions: (1) Draw a connecting line from each two words on the left to the corresponding compound word on the right.

cow boy   herself

her self   cowboy

birth day   popcorn

pop corn   birthday

Directions: (1) Read each compound word. (2) Divide each compound word and write the two separate words. (3) Reread the completed paper going across.

1. herself = _____

2. birthday = _____

3. popcorn = _____

4. cowboy = _____

Name:

COMPOUND WORD PUZZLE

Directions: Cut out the words below and paste them under the correct pictures to form compound words.

- cut -

| cup | snow | cow | bird | tea | sail |
| boat | house | man | pot | boy | cake |

COMPOUND WORDS

Directions: Draw a line from each word on the left to a word on the right to make a compound word. Then write each compound word in the last column.

news	noon	1. newspaper
after	shine	2.
mail	paper	3.
barn	man	4.
sun	yard	5.
home	plane	6.
any	work	7.
air	thing	8.

COMPOUND WORDS

Directions: Draw a line from each word on the left to a word on the right to make a compound word. Then write each compound word in the last column.

in	by	1.
good	ball	2.
cow	side	3.
foot	boy	4.
out	day	5.
high	doors	6.
to	way	7.
some	one	8.

Name:

COMPOUND WORDS

Directions: Read the story and list the compound words below.

Jeff went outside to play football with Mike. When he got to Mike's house, he saw a baseball on the sidewalk. He threw it into the backyard. Then he rang Mike's doorbell. Mike's grandfather came to the door and told Jeff that Mike wasn't inside the house. He had gone to the playground without Jeff and was waiting for him there.

1.
2.
3.
4.
5.
6.
7.
8.
9.
10.

COMPOUND WORD PUZZLE

Directions: Write the correct words in the blank spaces to form compound words.

Name: _____

COMPOUND WORDS

Be careful!

Directions: Divide and circle each compound word.

1. doorbell
2. under
3. hatbox
4. basket
5. raincoat
6. sunflower
7. playing
8. driveway
9. windmill
10. began
11. upset
12. cannot
13. return
14. himself
15. teacher
16. toothbrush

Name: _____

COMPOUND WORDS

Directions: Add a word after each word to make a compound word. Ex. may be.

1. mail _____
2. some _____
3. no _____
4. with _____
5. in _____
6. every _____
7. out _____
8. foot _____
9. bed _____
10. to _____
11. any _____
12. bird _____

Name: _____

POSSESSIVE

To show that someone (or something) owns (or possesses) something, add **'s** to the word. This is called "apostrophe s."

I own this car.

John's car

John

Directions: (1) Read each word. (2) Write each word with the ending "'s." (3) Read the new word you wrote. (4) Reread the completed paper going across.

1. John

2. Pat

3. Ted

4. Jill

5. Tom

6. Mother

7. Father

8. Baby

Name:

POSSESSIVE

To show that someone (or something) owns (or possesses) something, add **'s** to the word. This is called "apostrophe s."

This is my house.

dog's house

Directions: (1) Read each word. (2) Write each word with the ending "'s." (3) Read the new word you wrote. (4) Reread the completed paper going across.

1. boy
2. girl
3. cat
4. dog
5. man
6. woman
7. pet
8. friend

Name:

POSSESSIVE

When a person's name ends in <u>s</u>, add just the apostrophe.

This belongs to me. — Thomas' kite

<u>Directions</u>: (1) Read each word. (2) Write each word with the ending "'." (3) Read the new word you wrote. (4) Reread the completed paper going across.

1. Thomas
2. Gus
3. Kris
4. Charles
5. Niles
6. Ross
7. Marcus
8. Jesus

Name:

POSSESSIVE

Directions: Make each object below belong to someone in your class by writing the person's name before the word. If the name ends in "s," add just the "'." Then reread the completed paper.

dress	Diana's dress
pencil	
cat	
turtle	
top	
book	
ball	
desk	

Name: _____

POSSESSIVE

Directions: Give something to each somebody below and show possession by adding "'s" to the name (or just "'" if the name ends in "s").

Ex. Kristine — Kristine's book

Kristine
"I like my book."

Fred	clown
Rose	duck
Ken	kitten
Jan	doll
Gus	fish
Pam	lady

Name:

POSSESSIVE

"Do you like my hat?"

Caroline

Directions: Write the possessive of each statement as in the following example. Then reread the completed paper going across.

Ex. The hat of Caroline — Caroline's hat

1. The ball of Ted
2. The book of Pat
3. The car of Tom
4. The doll of Jill
5. The truck of James
6. The desk of Sue

Name: _____

75

POSSESSIVE

Directions: Write the possessive of each statement as in the following example. Then reread the completed paper going across.

Ex. The dish of the cat — The cat's dish

Where is my dish?
cat

1. The bat of the boy _____

2. The pen of the girl _____

3. The bone of the dog _____

4. The hat of the man _____

5. The roof of the house _____

6. The tail of the fox _____

Name: _____

POSSESSIVE

This is my new record.

Mark

Directions: Write the possessive of each statement as in the following example. Then reread the completed paper going across.

Ex. Mark has a new record. — It is Mark's record.

1. Maria can ride her bike.   It is _____ bike.

2. The dog found a bone.   It is the _____.

3. Tom has a new pet.   It is _____.

4. Betty likes her doll.   It is _____.

5. Mother made a cake.   It is _____.

6. The clown lost his hat.   It is the _____.

76

Name: _____

POSSESSIVE

This is the men's store.

This is the boys' ball.

When something belongs to more than one person or thing, show possession the same way you do when something belongs to just one person or thing.

If the word doesn't end in "s," add "'s."	If the word does end in "s," add just "'."
children	boys
men	girls
women	wives
people	husbands
cattle	neighbors
oxen	clubs

Name: _____

POSSESSIVE

Directions: Write in all the apostrophes where they belong in the following sentences.

1. The clowns and bears are in Dans show.

2. The boys goat has Marys doll.

3. How many books are the wives books?

4. The kittens box is full of toys.

5. The fish and cats are eating James food.

6. Three ducks jumped into Sallys pool.

Name: _____

POSSESSIVE

Directions: Write in all the apostrophes where they belong in the following sentences.

1. The girls shoes are red.
2. The childrens toys are in the box.
3. The dogs will bark at Pats cats.
4. The ladys hat is on Bettys table.
5. Thomas ball is on top of Bills roof.
6. The babys bottle is on Dots lap.

Name: _____

CONTRACTIONS

A contraction is a short way of saying two words. It is written by putting the two words together and leaving out one or more letters. An apostrophe (') is put in place of the missing letters.

not

Two Words	Contraction	Missing Letters	Two Words	Contraction	Missing Letters
is not	isn't	o	do not	don't	o
did not	didn't		does not	doesn't	
can not	can't		has not	hasn't	
was not	wasn't		were not	weren't	
have not	haven't		could not	couldn't	
are not	aren't		would not	wouldn't	

80

Name: _____

CONTRACTIONS
not

Directions: (1) Connect each two words with the corresponding contraction. (2) Write the two words for each contraction. (3) Read the completed paper.

is not   can't

did not   isn't

can not   haven't

have not   didn't

1. can't = _____

2. isn't = _____

3. haven't = _____

4. didn't = _____

Name: _____

CONTRACTIONS

Can you write the contraction?

Directions: (1) Read each two words. (2) Write the contraction in column 2 and the missing letters in column 3. (3) Reread the completed paper going across.

not

Two Words	Contraction	Missing Letters	Two Words	Contraction	Missing Letters
was not			is not		
are not			have not		
has not			did not		
were not			does not		
should not			can not		
had not			could not		

82

Name: _____

CONTRACTIONS

A contraction is a short way of saying two words. It is written by putting the two words together and leaving out one or more letters. An apostrophe (') is put in place of the missing letters.

will

Two Words	Contraction	Missing Letters
I will	I'll	
you will	you'll	
he will	he'll	
she will	she'll	
we will	we'll	
they will	they'll	

have-has

Two Words	Contraction	Missing Letters
I have	I've	
you have	you've	
we have	we've	
they have	they've	
he has	he's	
she has	she's	

Name: _____

CONTRACTIONS
have - has

Directions: (1) Connect each two words with the corresponding contraction. (2) Write the two words for each contraction. (3) Read the completed paper.

we have	I've
he has	we've
I have	she's
she has	he's

1. we've = _____

2. he's = _____

3. I've = _____

4. she's = _____

CONTRACTIONS

Name: _____

Directions: (1) Read each two words. (2) Write the contraction in column 2 and the missing letters in column 3. (3) Reread the completed paper going across.

will

Two Words	Contraction	Missing Letters
he will		
they will		
you will		
it will		
we will		
I will		

have - has

Two Words	Contraction	Missing Letters
you have		
I have		
he has		
they have		
we have		
she has		

86

Name: _____

CONTRACTIONS

A contraction is a short way of saying two words. It is written by putting the two words together and leaving out one or more letters. An apostrophe (') is put in place of the missing letters.

is

Two Words	Contraction	Missing Letters	Two Words	Contraction	Missing Letters
it is	it's		here is	here's	
she is	she's		there is	there's	
he is	he's		where is	where's	
that is	that's		what is	what's	
who is	who's		how is	how's	

Directions: Read each two words and the contraction. Then write the missing letters in the next column.

CONTRACTIONS
is

Directions: (1) Connect each two words with the corresponding contraction. (2) Write the two words for each contraction. (3) Read the completed paper.

that is   who's

he is   it's

it is   he's

who is   that's

1. it's   = _____

2. he's   = _____

3. who's   = _____

4. that's = _____

CONTRACTIONS

Directions: (1) Read each two words. (2) Write the contraction in column 2 and the missing letters in column 3. (3) Reread the completed paper going across.

is

Two Words	Contraction	Missing Letters	Two Words	Contraction	Missing Letters
here is			that is		
it is			he is		
she is			what is		
where is			how is		
there is			who is		
why is			when is		

Name: _____

CONTRACTIONS

A contraction is a short way of saying two words. It is written by putting the two words together and leaving out one or more letters. An apostrophe (') is put in place of the missing letters.

am – are

Two Words	Contraction	Missing Letters
I am	I'm	
You are	you're	
we are	we're	
they are	they're	

would

Two Words	Contraction	Missing Letters
I would	I'd	
you would	you'd	
he would	he'd	
she would	she'd	
we would	we'd	
they would	they'd	

us

let us	let's	

90

Name:
CONTRACTIONS
would

Directions: (1) Connect each two words with the corresponding contraction. (2) Write the two words for each contraction. (3) Read the completed paper.

I would	they'd
he would	you'd
they would	I'd
you would	he'd

1. you'd = _____
2. I'd = _____
3. he'd = _____
4. they'd = _____

Name: _____

CONTRACTIONS

Directions: (1) Read each two words. (2) Write the missing letters in column 2 and the contraction in column 3. (3) Reread the completed paper going across.

am – are

Two Words	Missing Letters	Contraction
you are		
they are		
we are		
I am		
let us		us

would

Two Words	Missing Letters	Contraction
we would		
she would		
he would		
I would		
you would		
they would		

94

Name:

CONTRACTIONS REVIEW

Two Words	Contraction	Contraction	Two Words
1. I will		7. isn't	
2. can not		8. we'll	
3. they have		9. you've	
4. you would		10. she's	
5. I am		11. let's	
6. that is		12. they're	

Name: _____

CONTRACTIONS
REVIEW

Two Words	Contraction		Contraction	Two Words
1. you are		7. I'd		
2. he has		8. it's		
3. let us		9. won't		
4. did not		10. we've		
5. they will		11. you're		
6. he would		12. I'm		

96

Name: _____

ADD-A-PREFIX

A Prefix is placed <u>before</u> a word to form a new word.

<u>Directions</u>: (1) Read each word. (2) Write each word, adding the Prefix. (3) Read the new word you wrote. (4) Reread the completed paper going across.

un

1. fair   unfair
2. true   _____
3. lock   _____
4. able   _____
5. tie   _____
6. happy   _____
7. afraid   _____
8. just   _____

en

1. joy   _____
2. danger   _____
3. force   _____
4. rich   _____
5. trust   _____
6. circle   _____
7. large   _____
8. close   _____

For superstars only

<u>Increase Your Vocabulary</u>
Can you figure out the meanings of the new words you wrote?

un - not, the opposite of
en - to cover or surround with

Name:
ADD-A-PREFIX

A Prefix is placed <u>before</u> a word to form a new word.

<u>Directions</u>: (1) Read each word. (2) Write each word, adding the Prefix. (3) Read the new word you wrote. (4) Reread the completed paper going across.

re

1. turn _____
2. place _____
3. new _____
4. write _____
5. visit _____
6. fresh _____
7. gain _____
8. fill _____

de

1. rail _____
2. tour _____
3. frost _____
4. throne _____
5. part _____
6. code _____
7. grade _____
8. value _____

For superstars only

<u>Increase Your Vocabulary</u>
Can you figure out the meanings of the new words you wrote?

re - again, once more
de - away from, the opposite

Name:

FIND THE PREFIX

Directions: Read each word. Then write the root of the word in the second column and the prefix in the third column.

Root + Prefix	Root	Prefix
1. rerun		
2. enable		
3. unload		
4. rebuild		
5. demerit		
6. unkind		
7. enact		
8. deface		

ADD-A-PREFIX

A Prefix is placed before a word to form a new word.

Directions: (1) Read each word. (2) Write each word, adding the Prefix. (3) Read the new word you wrote. (4) Reread the completed paper going across.

mis

1. take _____
2. print _____
3. deed _____
4. fit _____
5. treat _____
6. use _____
7. spell _____
8. lead _____

dis

1. like _____
2. agree _____
3. appear _____
4. own _____
5. obey _____
6. please _____
7. color _____
8. locate _____

For superstars only

Increase Your Vocabulary
Can you figure out the meanings of the new words you wrote?

mis - bad or wrong
dis - not, the opposite of

ADD-A-PREFIX

A Prefix is placed before a word to form a new word.

Directions: (1) Read each word. (2) Write each word, adding the Prefix. (3) Read the new word you wrote. (4) Reread the completed paper going across.

in___

1. correct _____
2. direct _____
3. formal _____
4. active _____
5. justice _____
6. secure _____
7. visible _____
8. definite _____

im___

1. proper _____
2. polite _____
3. perfect _____
4. mature _____
5. movable _____
6. patient _____
7. modest _____
8. mobile _____

For superstars only

Increase Your Vocabulary
Can you figure out the meanings of the new words you wrote?

in- not, lack of
im- not, lack of

FIND THE PREFIX

Directions: Read each word. Then write the root of the word in the second column and the prefix in the third column.

Root + Prefix	Root	Prefix
1. immortal		
2. misjudge		
3. inattention		
4. dissatisfy		
5. misstate		
6. impersonal		
7. disorder		
8. incomplete		

ADD-A-PREFIX

A Prefix is placed before a word to form a new word.

Directions: (1) Read each word. (2) Write each word, adding the Prefix. (3) Read the new word you wrote. (4) Reread the completed paper going across.

pre

1. fix _____
2. heat _____
3. pay _____
4. view _____
5. war _____
6. date _____
7. judge _____
8. paid _____

sub

1. way _____
2. soil _____
3. title _____
4. group _____
5. marine _____
6. topic _____
7. sonic _____
8. divide _____

For Superstars only

Increase Your Vocabulary
Can you figure out the meanings of the new words you wrote?

pre - before
sub - under, below

Name: _____

ADD- A - PREFIX

A Prefix is placed <u>before</u> a word to form a new word.

<u>Directions</u>: (1) Read each word. (2) Write each word, adding the Prefix. (3) Read the new word you wrote. (4) Reread the completed paper going across.

bi

1. weekly _____
2. monthly _____
3. annual _____
4. cycle _____
5. focal _____
6. lingual _____
7. cuspid _____
8. linear _____

semi

1. annual _____
2. circle _____
3. darkness _____
4. final _____
5. formal _____
6. colon _____
7. conscious _____
8. precious _____

For Superstars only

<u>Increase Your Vocabulary</u>
Can you figure out the meanings of the new words you wrote?

bi-   two, every two
semi-   half, partly

103

ADD-A-PREFIX

A Prefix is placed <u>before</u> a word to form a new word.

<u>Directions</u>: (1) Read each word. (2) Write each word, adding the Prefix. (3) Read the new word you wrote. (4) Reread the completed paper going across.

mid

1. night _____
2. way _____
3. air _____
4. summer _____

non

1. profit _____
2. skid _____
3. sense _____
4. stop _____

fore

1. head _____
2. see _____
3. arm _____
4. tell _____

anti

1. freeze _____
2. trust _____
3. body _____
4. social _____

For Superstars only

<u>Increase</u> <u>Your</u> <u>Vocabulary</u>
Can you figure out the meanings of the new words you wrote?

mid - in the middle part of
fore - in front, before
non - without
anti - against, opposed

Name:

FIND THE PREFIX

Directions: Read each word. Then write the root of the word in the second column and the prefix in the third column.

Root + Prefix	Root	Prefix
1. semitropical		
2. nonliving		
3. prehistoric		
4. foreground		
5. subside		
6. bilateral		
7. midstream		
8. anticlimax		

WRITE A PREFIX

Directions: Add a prefix to each word to form a new word. Then reread the completed paper.

un	en	re	de	mis

1. __mis__ take
2. ___ frost
3. ___ turn
4. ___ fair
5. ___ deed
6. ___ joy

dis	in	im	pre	sub	bi

1. ___ fix
2. ___ correct
3. ___ way
4. ___ polite
5. ___ like
6. ___ weekly

semi	mid	non	fore	anti

1. ___ night
2. ___ head
3. ___ circle
4. ___ profit
5. ___ way
6. ___ body

Name: _____

ADD-A-SUFFIX

A Suffix is placed <u>after</u> a word to form a new word.

<u>Directions</u>: (1) Read each word. (2) Write each word, adding the Suffix. (3) Read the new word you wrote. (4) Reread the completed paper going across.

<u>less</u>

1. care   <u>careless</u>
2. use   _____
3. help   _____
4. fear   _____
5. pain   _____
6. color   _____
7. harm   _____
8. need   _____

<u>ness</u>

1. kind   _____
2. still   _____
3. good   _____
4. dark   _____
5. great   _____
6. bright _____
7. neat   _____
8. ill   _____

★ For Superstars only

<u>Increase</u> <u>Your</u> <u>Vocabulary</u>
Can you figure out the meanings of the new words you wrote?

less – without, lacking
ness – condition or quality of being

ADD-A-SUFFIX

A Suffix is placed <u>after</u> a word to form a new word.

Directions: (1) Read each word. (2) Write each word, adding the suffix. (3) Read the new word you wrote. (4) Reread the completed paper going across.

ish

1. child _____
2. boy _____
3. girl _____
4. fool _____
5. green _____
6. clown _____
7. sheep _____
8. sweet _____

able

1. enjoy _____
2. wash _____
3. suit _____
4. agree _____
5. break _____
6. port _____
7. pay _____
8. profit _____

For Superstars only

Increase Your Vocabulary
Can you figure out the meanings of the new words you wrote?

ish - resembling, having the character of
able - fit to be, worthy to be

FIND THE SUFFIX

Name: _____

Directions: Read each word. Then write the root of the word in the second column and the suffix in the third column.

Root + Suffix	Root	Suffix
1. friendless		
2. dependable		
3. softness		
4. ghoulish		
5. thoughtless		
6. acceptable		
7. directness		
8. squirmish		

Name: _____

ADD-A-SUFFIX

A suffix is placed <u>after</u> a word to form a new word.

<u>Directions</u>: (1) Read each word. (2) Write each word, adding the suffix. (3) Read the new word you wrote. (4) Reread the completed paper going across.

<u>ward</u>

1. after _____
2. back _____
3. up _____
4. out _____
5. side _____
6. down _____
7. in _____
8. home _____

<u>ment</u>

1. pave _____
2. base _____
3. state _____
4. ship _____
5. agree _____
6. excite _____
7. punish _____
8. enroll _____

★ For Superstars only

<u>Increase Your Vocabulary</u>
Can you figure out the meanings of the new words you wrote?

ward – in the direction of
ment – the act or state of being

Name:

ADD-A-SUFFIX

A suffix is placed <u>after</u> a word to form a new word.

Directions: (1) Read each word. (2) Write each word, adding the suffix. (3) Read the new word you wrote. (4) Reread the completed paper going across.

<u>ship</u>

1. hard _____
2. court _____
3. fellow _____
4. friend _____
5. leader _____
6. king _____
7. lord _____
8. town _____

<u>hood</u>

1. child _____
2. boy _____
3. adult _____
4. man _____
5. girl _____
6. knight _____
7. false _____
8. neighbor _____

For superstars only

<u>Increase Your Vocabulary</u>
Can you figure out the meanings of the new words you wrote?

ship - condition or quality of
hood - state, quality of being

Name: _____

FIND THE SUFFIX

Directions: Read each word. Then write the root of the word in the second column and the suffix in the third column.

Root + Suffix	Root	Suffix
1. friendship		
2. childhood		
3. westward		
4. settlement		
5. hardship		
6. agreement		
7. northward		
8. falsehood		

Name: _____

SUFFIXES

A suffix is placed <u>after</u> a word to form a new word.

Directions: (1) Read each word. (2) Write each word, adding the suffix. (3) Read the new word you wrote. (4) Reread the completed paper going across.

<u>**ant**</u>	<u>**ist**</u>	<u>**age**</u>
assist _____	art _____	pass _____
defend _____	motor _____	post _____
expect _____	solo _____	drain _____
resist _____	violin _____	mile _____

For Superstars only

Increase Your Vocabulary

Can you figure out the meanings of the new words you wrote?

ant— doing, or that which does a certain thing
ist— one who makes a practice of doing
age— an act, process or result

Name: _____

SUFFIXES

A Suffix is placed <u>after</u> a word to form a new word.

<u>Directions:</u> (1) Read each word. (2) Write each word, adding the <u>Suffix</u>. (3) Read the new word you wrote. (4) Reread the completed paper.

some

tire _____

lone _____

whole _____

win _____

ous

joy _____

danger _____

mountain _____

poison _____

ance

appear _____

disturb _____

accept _____

assist _____

<u>Increase Your Vocabulary</u>

Can you figure out the meanings of the new words you wrote?

some — showing a tendency to
ous — full of, of the nature of
ance — state, quality or condition

★ For Superstars only

Name:
FIND THE SUFFIX

Directions: Read each word. Then write the root of the word in the second column and the suffix in the third column.

Root + Suffix	Root	Suffix
1. appearance		
2. harpist		
3. cumbersome		
4. spoilage		
5. resistant		
6. prosperous		
7. breakage		
8. organist		

ADD-A-DOUBLE SUFFIX

A Suffix is placed <u>after</u> a word to form a new word.

Directions: (1) Read each word. (2) Write each word, adding the suffix. (3) Read the new word you wrote. (4) Reread the completed paper going across.

<u>fully</u>

1. care _____
2. hope _____
3. faith _____
4. thought _____
5. skill _____
6. cheer _____
7. truth _____
8. play _____

<u>fulness</u>

1. use _____
2. grace _____
3. help _____
4. bash _____
5. thank _____
6. rest _____
7. forget _____
8. hope _____

★ For Superstars only

<u>Increase Your Vocabulary</u>
Can you figure out the meanings of the new words you wrote?

ly – having the nature of

Name:

SUFFIXES

A suffix is placed after a word to form a new word.

Directions: (1) Read each word. (2) Write each word, adding a suffix. (3) Read the new word you wrote. (4) Reread the completed paper.

ishness

fool _____
girl _____
boy _____
child _____
squirm _____
gray _____

ening

fright _____
hard _____
quick _____
soft _____
tight _____
sharp _____

ingly

long _____
seem _____
charm _____
last _____
will _____
alarm _____

Name: _____

WRITE A SUFFIX

Directions: Add a suffix to each word to form a new word. Then reread the completed paper.

| less | ness | ish | able |

1. bottom _less_
2. comfort _____
3. sore _____
4. service _____
5. fool _____
6. end _____

| ward | ment | ship | hood | ant |

1. pay _____
2. lord _____
3. woman _____
4. down _____
5. descend _____
6. friend _____

| ist | age | some | ous | ance |

1. danger _____
2. post _____
3. art _____
4. bond _____
5. tire _____
6. appear _____

Name: _____

	Root	Prefix	Suffix
unplayful			
reprinted			
prefixes			
biweekly			
unuseable			
enlargement			
retesting			
unwholesome			

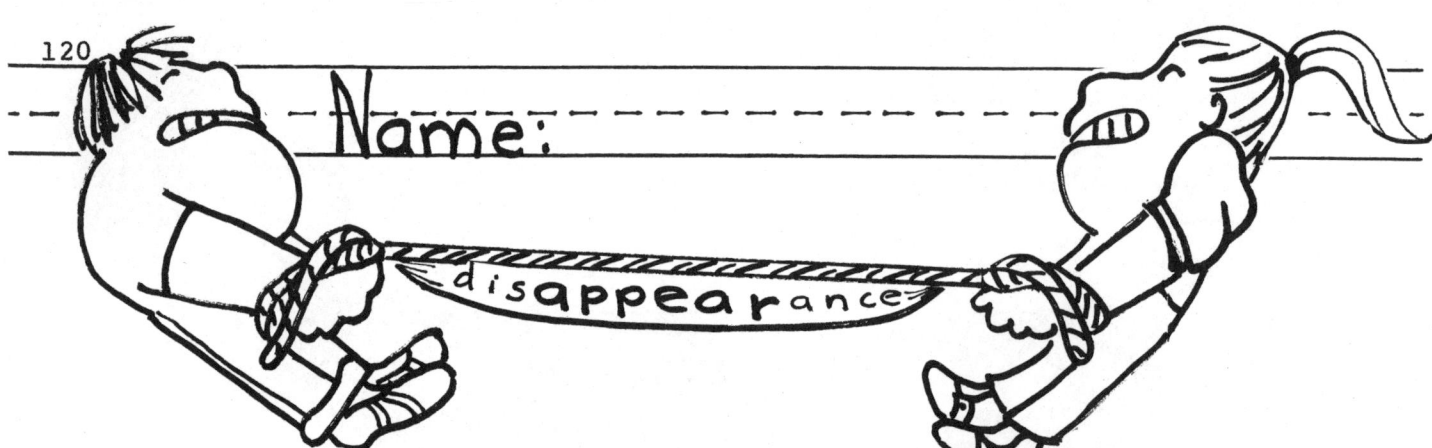

Name: _____

	Root	Prefix	Suffix
disappearance			
unjoyous			
refreshing			
impolitely			
detoured			
enrichment			
refiller			
nonprofitable			

Name: _____

	Root	Prefix	Suffix
endangering			
disagreement			
misspelled			
departing			
unchangeable			
informally			
disarmed			
indirectness			

SYLLABLES

Words can be broken down into separate sounds. These separate sounds are called "syllables."
Clap your hands to each sound as you pronounce the following words and write the number of syllables (or sounds) you hear in each word.

	How Many Syllables?		How Many Syllables?
star	1	pumpkin	___
flower	___	cat	___
clown	___	valentine	___
elephant	___	pencil	___
helicopter	___	butterfly	___
fruit	___	automobile	___

Name: _____

SYLLABLES

The syllables in words are like the beats in music. Clap your hands to each sound as you pronounce the following words and write the number of syllables (or sounds) you hear in each word.

	How Many Syllables?		How Many Syllables?
 piano	___	 hat	___
 television	___	 alligator	___
 sweater	___	 turkey	___
 lollipop	___	 envelope	___
 kite	___	 ball	___
 dish	___	 turtle	___

SYLLABLES
Clap - Say - Write

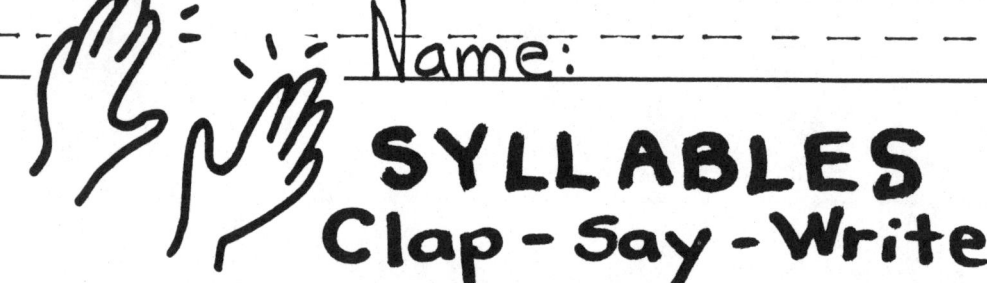

Directions: Clap your hands to each sound as you pronounce each of the following words. Then write the word in the column which tells how many syllables there are in the word.

go	children	run	began	another
under	find	interest	afternoon	happy
together	because	make	come	wonderful

1 Syllable	2 Syllables	3 Syllables

Name: _____

SYLLABLES + ACCENT MARKS

When you pronounce a word with more than one syllable, one syllable is usually said with more force or emphasis.

    Ex.   be GIN   EN ter   re MEM ber

This is called the "accented" syllable. An accent mark like this "/" is put over the end of the accented syllable to show that it receives more stress.

    Ex.   be gin'   en'ter   re mem'ber

Pronounce each of the following two-syllable words and put an accent mark over the end of the accented syllable:

be gin'	for get	en joy
af ter	bet ter	hap py
li on	pen cil	to day
in side	with out	bal loon
un lock	din ner	can dle

Name: _____

SYLLABLES + ACCENT MARKS

Directions: Pronounce each of the following words and put an accent mark over the end of the accented syllable.

Two-Syllable Words

1. un' der
2. kit chen
3. o ver
4. mar ket
5. un til
6. hun gry
7. sur prise
8. chil dren
9. win dow
10. be gan

Three-Syllable Words

1. but ter fly
2. to geth er
3. in ter est
4. val en tine
5. an oth er
6. el e phant
7. lol li pop
8. won der ful
9. im por tant
10. en vel ope

Name:

SYLLABLES + ACCENT MARKS

Directions: Pronounce each of the following words and put an accent mark over the end of the accented syllable.

Three-Syllable Words

1. hap pi ly
2. be gin ner
3. sud den ly
4. chim pan zee
5. vol ca no

6. en ter tain
7. car pen ter
8. va ca tion
9. dis con nect
10. ex act ly

Four-Syllable Words

1. hel i cop ter
2. a bil i ty
3. au to mo bile
4. cer tif i cate
5. ab so lute ly

6. lo co mo tive
7. tes ti mo ny
8. pop u la tion
9. di rec to ry
10. rev o lu tion

Name: _____

SYLLABLES

Rule 1: Divide between the double consonant.

Directions: Divide and accent each word below as in the example:

1. Clap + Say	2. Divide	3. Accent
happy	better	dinner
hap´·py		
ribbon	yellow	swimmer
	puzzle	letter

128

Name: _____

SYLLABLES

Rule 1: Divide between the double consonant.

Directions: Divide and accent each word below as follows: 1. Clap + Say  2. Divide  3. Accent

bigger	rubber	grinning	balloon
tennis	winner	slipper	jolly
ladder	hopping	puppet	stopping

Name: _____

SYLLABLES

Rule 2: Divide between the unlike consonants.

<u>Directions:</u> Divide and accent each word below as in the example:

1. Clap + Say   2. Divide   3. Accent

window	sister	carpet	velvet
wín'dow			
picture	number	pencil	garden

Name: _____

SYLLABLES

Rule 2: Divide between the unlike consonants.

Directions: Divide and accent each word below as follows: 1. Clap + say   2. Divide   3. Accent

candy	winter	circus	market
mister	finger	whisper	basket
corner	wonder	monkey	thunder

Name: _____

SYLLABLES

Rule 3: The consonant joins the "le."

Directions: Divide and accent each word below as in the example:

1. Clap + Say | 2. Divide | 3. Accent

purple	candle	people	tumble
pur´ ple			
jungle	simple	turtle	single

Name: _____

SYLLABLES

Rule 3: The consonant joins the "le."

Directions: Divide and accent each word below as follows:

1. Clap + Say
2. Divide
3. Accent

dimple	thistle	poodle	temple
ramble	sample	marble	kindle
steeple	mingle	fumble	bungle

Name: _____

SYLLABLES

Rule 4: Divide between the root and ending.

Directions: Divide and accent each word below as in the example:

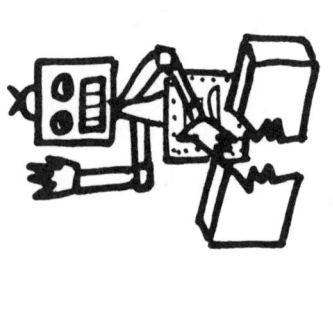

1. Clap + Say	2. Divide	3. Accent
wanted	going	lucky
wánt/ed	old/er	
brighten	dresses	playful friendly

Name: _____

SYLLABLES

Rule 4: Divide between the root and ending.

Directions: Divide and accent each word below as follows: 1. Clap + Say 2. Divide 3. Accent

thankful	started	looking	softer
rainy	golden	boxes	highest
kindness	childish	really	careless

Name:

SYLLABLES

Rule 5: Divide between compound words.

Directions: Divide and accent each word below as in the example:

1. Clap + Say 2. Divide 3. Accent

see saw | cow boy | some one | with out

sēe´saw

be side | in to | foot ball | to day

Name: _____

SYLLABLES

Rule 5: Divide between compound words.

Directions: Divide and accent each word below as follows:

1. Clap + Say
2. Divide
3. Accent

may/be	base/ball	home/work	rail/road
her/self	mail/box	barn/yard	post/man
in/side	some/thing	good/by	out/doors

138

Name:

SYLLABLE REVIEW

Directions: Divide and accent each of the following words.

Divide between the double consonant.

puzzle	happy	letter	balloon
púz´zle			

Divide between the unlike consonants.

candy	window	garden	number

The consonant joins the "le."

people	candle	trouble	purple

Divide between the root and ending.

going	lucky	wanted	golden

Divide between compound words.

without	into	someone	beside

Name: _____

SYLLABLES

Rule 1: Divide between the double consonant.

Directions: Divide and accent each word below as follows:

1. Clap + say  2. Divide 3. Accent

sudden	pillow	follow	muffin
batter	summer	happen	supper
wettest	lesson	wiggle	matter

Name: _____

SYLLABLES

Rule 2: Divide between the unlike consonants.

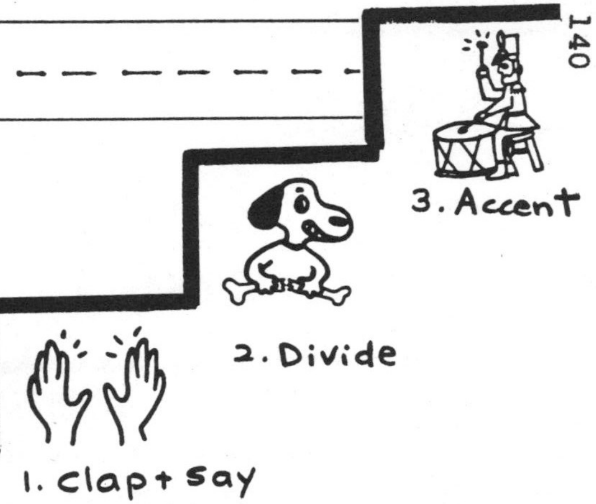

Directions: Divide and accent each word below as follows:
1. Clap + say
2. Divide
3. Accent

princess	distance	powder	filter
subject	turkey	donkey	plenty
problem	signal	curtain	splinter

Name: _____

SYLLABLES

Rule 3: The consonant joins the "le."

Directions: Divide and accent each word below as follows: 1. Clap + Say   2. Divide   3. Accent

circle	trouble	dangle	mumble
handle	startle	humble	thimble
gentle	scramble	whistle	noodle

Name: _____

SYLLABLES

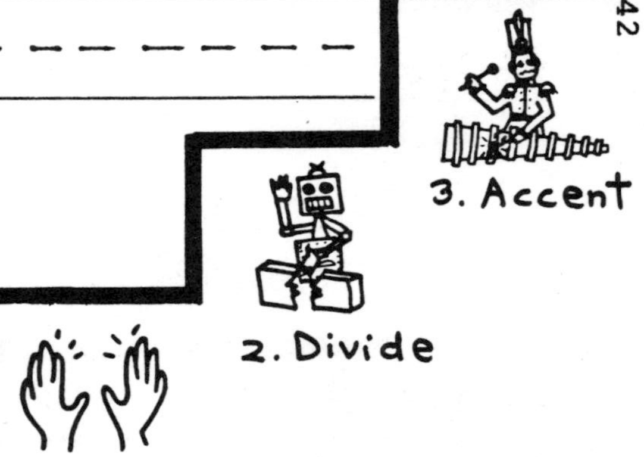

Rule 4: Divide between the root word and ending.

Directions: Divide and accent each word below as follows: 1. Clap + Say 2. Divide 3. Accent

waited	safely	talking	windy
artist	sharpen	sleepy	cleanest
homeward	kindness	payment	joyous

Name: _____

SYLLABLES

Rule 5: Divide between the compound words.

Directions: Divide and accent each word below as follows: 1. clap + say   2. Divide   3. Accent

sidewalk	raincoat	airplane	birdhouse
hatbox	toothbrush	starfish	playground
doorbell	hilltop	notebook	driveway

SYLLABLE REVIEW

Name: _____

Divide and accent each of the following words:

Divide between the double consonant

| winner | tennis | matter | lesson |

Divide between the unlike consonants.

| winter | picture | circus | sister |

The consonant joins the "le."

| steeple | turtle | poodle | single |

Divide between the root and ending.

| friendly | playful | highest | older |

Divide between compound words.

| cowboy | football | homework | sidewalk |

Name: _____

SYLLABLES

Rule 6: Don't split a Digraph or Blend.

Directions: Divide and accent each word below as in the example:

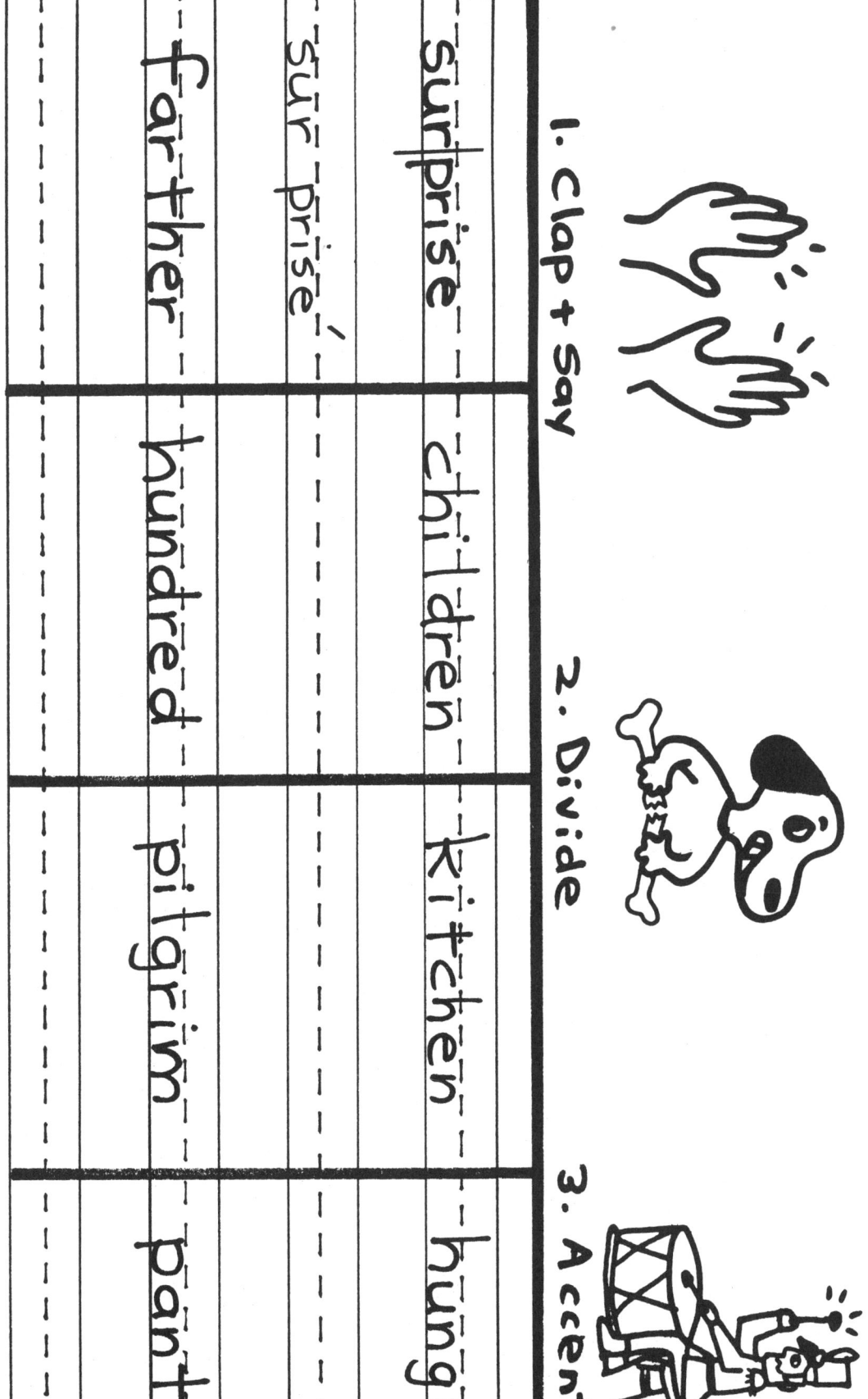

1. Clap + Say   2. Divide   3. Accent

sur|prise	children	kitchen	hungry
sur´prise			
farther	hundred	pilgrim	pantry

Name: _____

SYLLABLES

Rule 6: Don't split a Digraph or Blend.

<u>Directions:</u> Divide and accent each word below as follows:
1. Clap + say
2. Divide
3. Accent

control	purchase	subtract	congress
marshal	display	complete	distract
pastry	central	panther	wondrous

146

Name: _____

SYLLABLES

Rule 7: Divide after the long vowel.

Directions: Divide and accent each word below as in the example:

1. Clap + Say    2. Divide    3. Accent

mu´/sic

music	table	open	baby
paper	lion	tiger	broken

Name: _____

SYLLABLES

Rule 7: Divide after the long vowel.

Directions: Divide and accent each word below as follows:
1. Clap + Say 
2. Divide 
3. Accent 

secret	noble	pilot	bacon
final	motor	fever	diet
over	title	apron	lady

148

Name: _____

SYLLABLES

Rule 8: One vowel can be a syllable.

Directions: Divide and accent each word below as in the example:

1. Clap + Say    2. Divide    3. Accent

cap´i tal

cap i tal	president	hol i day	mag a zine
an i mal	tel e cast	hes i tate	eas i ly

Name: _____

SYLLABLES

3. Accent
2. Divide
1. Clap + Say

Rule 8: One vowel can be a syllable.

Directions: Divide and accent each word below as follows:

busily	educate	benefit	telephone
popular	vinegar	regular	monitor
crocodile	quality	catalog	skeleton

Name:

SYLLABLE REVIEW

Divide and accent each of the following words:

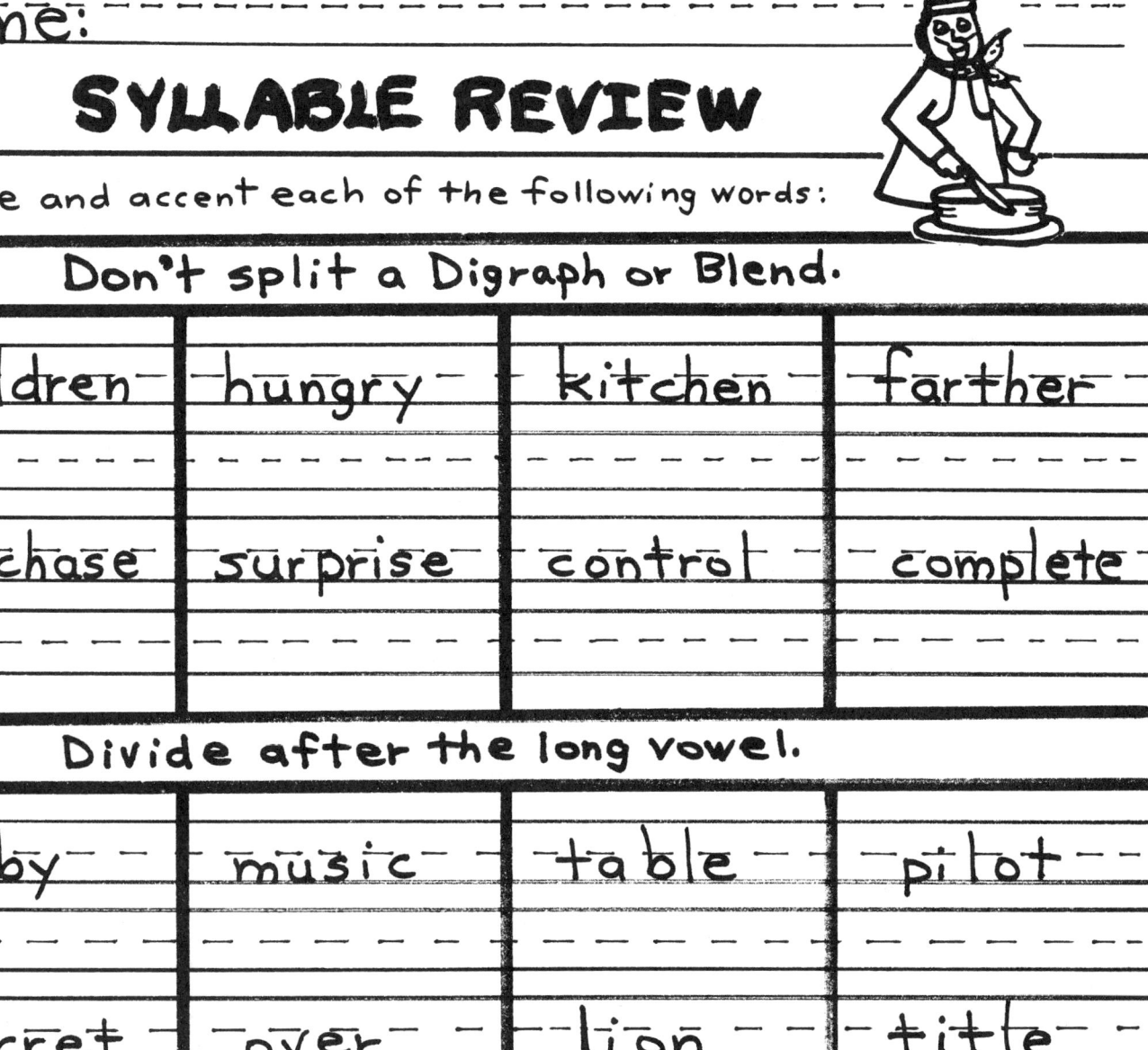

Don't split a Digraph or Blend.

children	hungry	kitchen	farther
purchase	surprise	control	complete

Divide after the long vowel.

baby	music	table	pilot
secret	over	lion	title

One vowel can be a syllable.

holiday	magazine	telecast	lovable
skeleton	capital	animal	president

Name: _____

SYLLABLES

Rule 6: Don't split a digraph or blend.

Directions: Divide and accent each word below as follows:
1. Clap + Say
2. Divide
3. Accent

152

merchant	dipthong	complain	membrane
belfry	substance	vestry	fulcrum
perplex	sentry	comply	paltry

Name: _____

SYLLABLES

Rule 7: Divide after the long vowel.

Directions: Divide and accent each word below as follows: 1. Clap + Say 2. Divide 3. Accent

moment	decide	maple	total
equal	nature	label	tiny
notice	silent	provide	famous

Name: _____

SYLLABLES

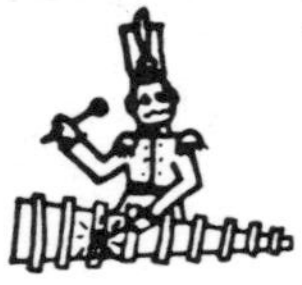

3. Accent
2. Divide 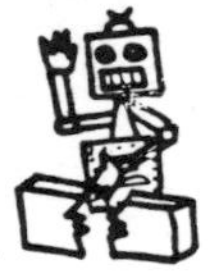
1. Clap + Say 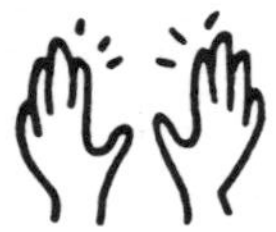

Rule 8: One vowel can be a syllable.

Directions: Divide and accent each word below as follows:

colony	maximum	imitate	edition
monument	taxation	dedicate	readiness
definite	magical	navigate	flexible

154

Name: _____ 155

SYLLABLE REVIEW

Can you remember the rules?

Directions: Divide and accent each of the following words.

sudden	airplane	noodle	tiger
kindness	popular	market	pantry
driveway	problem	follow	definite
windy	sample	merchant	paper

Name:

SYLLABLE REVIEW

Divide between the double consonant — 1

Divide between the unlike consonants. — 2

The consonant joins the "le." — 3

Divide between the root and ending. — 4

Directions: Divide and accent each word and write the number of the rule you applied. Ex. steeple - stee´ple - 3

	Divide and Accent	Which Rule?
1. ladder		
2. curly		
3. distance		
4. circle		
5. happen		
6. whistle		
7. joyful		
8. signal		

Name: _____

SYLLABLE REVIEW

5. Divide between the compound words.
6. Don't split a digraph or blend.
7. Divide after the long vowel.
8. One vowel can be a syllable.

Directions: Divide and accent each word and write the number of the rule you applied. Ex. music - mu´sic - 7

	Divide and Accent	Which Rule?
1. pilgrim		
2. inside		
3. lady		
4. imitate		
5. playground		
6. apron		
7. hundred		
8. maximum		

DICTIONARY
Diagram

Following are eight of the many features you will find when you look up a word in the dictionary:

Not every word in the dictionary will have every one of these features. However, you will find most of them in a Junior Dictionary.

Open your dictionary to any page and see how many of these features you can find next to each entry word.

ALPHABETIZING
(upper case)

ABCDEFGHIJKLMNOPQRSTUVWXYZ

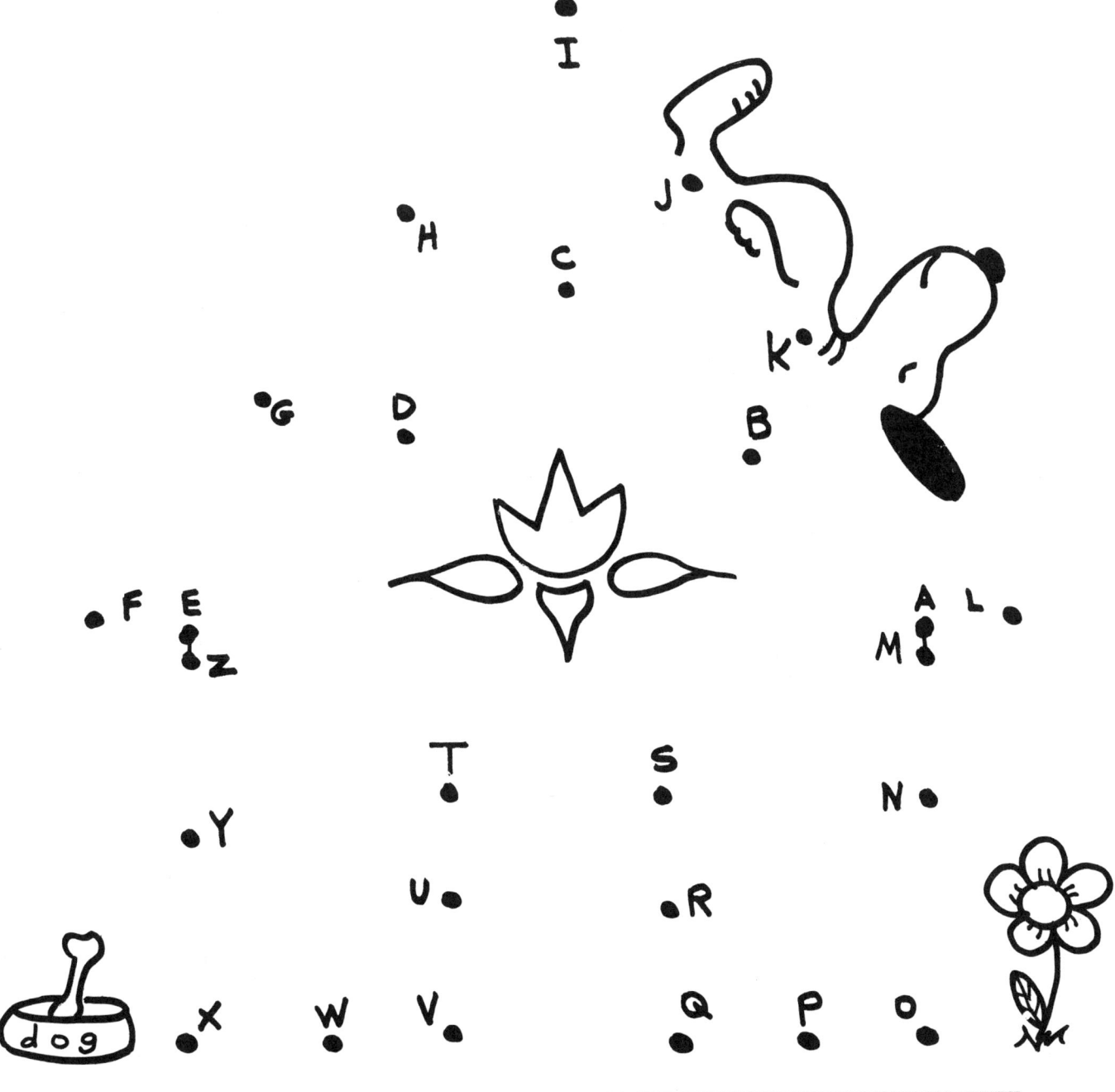

Follow the dots in alphabetical sequence, using the alphabet strip above as a guide.

ALPHABETIZING
(lower case)

abcdefghijklmnopqrstuvwxyz

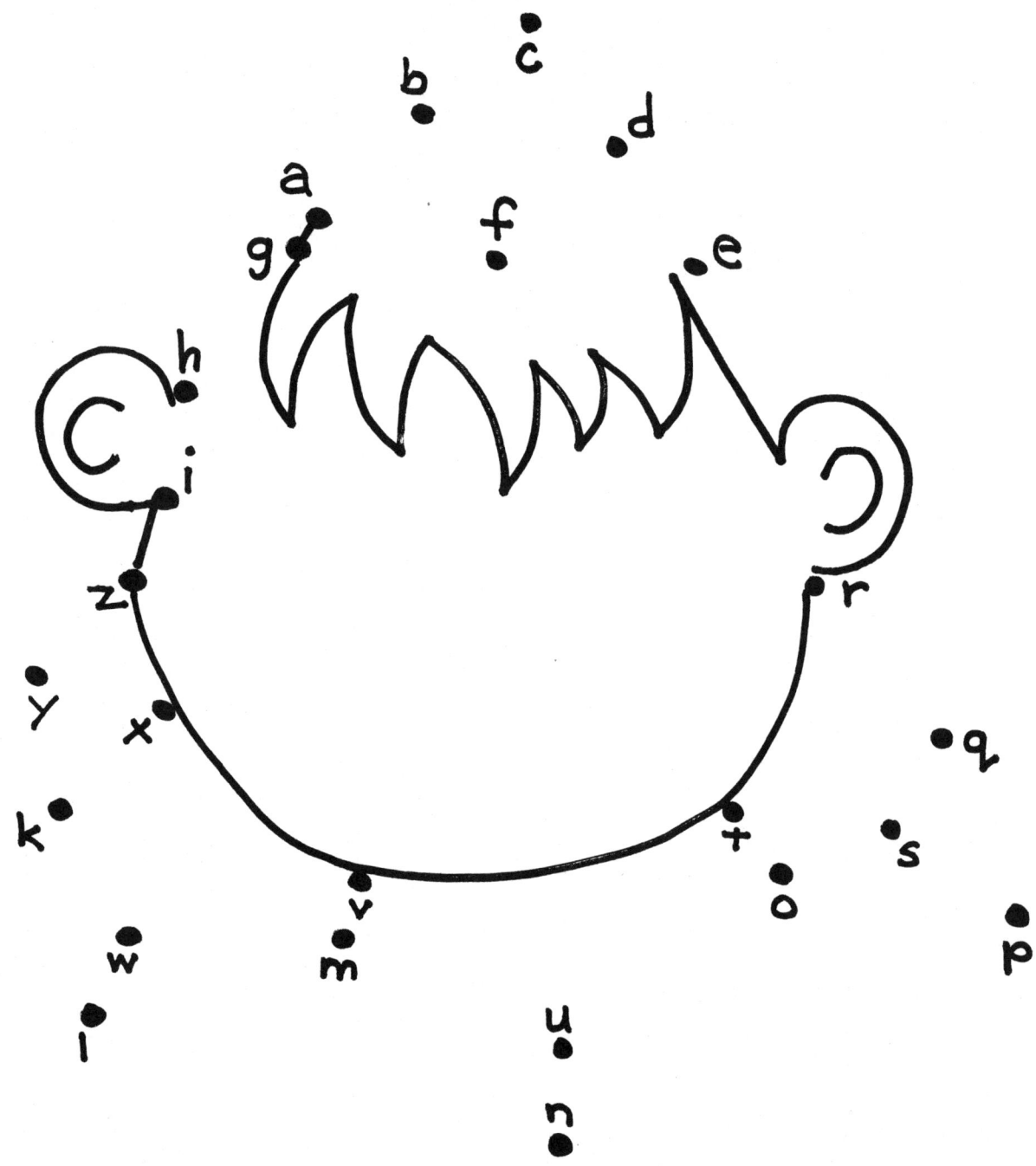

Follow the dots in alphabetical sequence, using the alphabet strip above as a guide. When you find out what the picture is, draw a funny face.

Name:

ALPHABETIZING

A B C D E F G H I J K L M N O P Q R S T U V W X Y Z
a b c d e f g h i j k l m n o p q r s t u v w x y z

Write in the missing capital letters.

A		C		E		G	H
	K		M		P		R
	T			W		Y	?

Write in the missing lower case letters.

	b		d		f	g		i
j		l		n	o		q	
s		u			x		z	?

ALPHABETIZING

A B C D E F G H I J K L M N O P Q R S T U V W X Y Z
a b c d e f g h i j k l m n o p q r s t u v w x y z

Write in the missing capital letters.

	B		D		F			I
J		L		N	O		Q	
S		U	V		X		Z	?

Write in the missing lower case letters.

a		c		e			h	
	k		m			p		r
	t		v	w		y		?

Name: _____

ALPHABETIZING

Write the letter that comes <u>after</u> each letter.

abcdefghijklmnopqrstuvwxyz

b _c_	p _	q _	i _	x _
e _	s _	t _	o _	d _
h _	v _	w _	l _	g _
k _	y _	c _	r _	j _
n _	a _	f _	u _	m _

Write the letter that comes <u>before</u> each letter.

_f_ g	_ v	_ d	_ n	_ z
_ j	_ y	_ o	_ k	_ c
_ m	_ b	_ r	_ q	_ i
_ p	_ e	_ u	_ t	_ f
_ s	_ h	_ x	_ w	_ l

Name:
ALPHABETIZING

Write the letters that come <u>before</u> and <u>after</u> each letter.

abcdefghijklmnopqrstuvwxyz

b	c	d
	f	
	n	
	d	
	k	
	i	

	p	
	s	
	j	
	u	
	y	
	m	

	l	
	e	
	r	
	t	
	x	
	b	

	v	
	q	
	o	
	h	
	g	
	w	

Write the letter that comes <u>between</u> each two letters.

d	b	c
m		o
h		j
d		f
o		q
j		l

l		n
b		d
i		k
p		r
e		g
r		t

f		h
k		m
c		e
n		p
g		i
q		s

u		w
s		u
v		x
x		z
t		v
w		y

Name:
ALPHABETIZING

Arrange each 3 letters in alphabetical order.

abcdefghijklmnopqrstuvwxyz

cba [a][b][c]   prq [ ][ ][ ]
fed [ ][ ][ ]   qsr [ ][ ][ ]
hgi [ ][ ][ ]   tus [ ][ ][ ]
jlk [ ][ ][ ]   wvx [ ][ ][ ]
nom [ ][ ][ ]   yzx [ ][ ][ ]

Arrange each 4 letters in alphabetical order.

tsvu [ ][ ][ ][ ]   knlm [ ][ ][ ][ ]
xwzy [ ][ ][ ][ ]   npmo [ ][ ][ ][ ]
bacd [ ][ ][ ][ ]   qrts [ ][ ][ ][ ]
gefh [ ][ ][ ][ ]   wxuv [ ][ ][ ][ ]
ljik [ ][ ][ ][ ]   xwyz [ ][ ][ ][ ]

ALPHABETIZING

Arrange each 5 letters in alphabetical order.

abcdefghijklmnopqrstuvwxyz

bcaed ☐☐☐☐☐   fihjg ☐☐☐☐☐
hjlik ☐☐☐☐☐   knmol ☐☐☐☐☐
vwxuy ☐☐☐☐☐   xvwzy ☐☐☐☐☐
gifjh ☐☐☐☐☐   egdfh ☐☐☐☐☐
moqnp ☐☐☐☐☐   rptsq ☐☐☐☐☐

Arrange each 6 letters in alphabetical order.

bdcfeg ☐☐☐☐☐☐   lnmpoq ☐☐☐☐☐☐
prsqtu ☐☐☐☐☐☐   cgedfh ☐☐☐☐☐☐
lpmonq ☐☐☐☐☐☐   uvxwzy ☐☐☐☐☐☐
dgiefh ☐☐☐☐☐☐   gkihlj ☐☐☐☐☐☐
jnlokm ☐☐☐☐☐☐   oqsptr ☐☐☐☐☐☐

Name: _____

ALPHABETIZING

Skip-a-Letter!

abcdefghijklmnopqrstuvwxyz

a d b		w u t x	
l i k		m l o p	
f d g		e c f g	
e h f		k i j m	
w z x		o p s r	

Skip-a-Letter or two!

c h a f j		e h b c j l	
i d g k e		u x r t v y	
l m k p s		g j m h p r	
g j h l m		u s x z v r	
u y w z t		i l f o q t	

Arrange each group of letters in alphabetical order. When letters of the alphabet are missing, just go on to the next letter in alphabetical order.

ALPHABETIZING

Write the capital letters of the alphabet.

Write the lower case letters of the alphabet.

Name: _____

ALPHABETIZING GAME

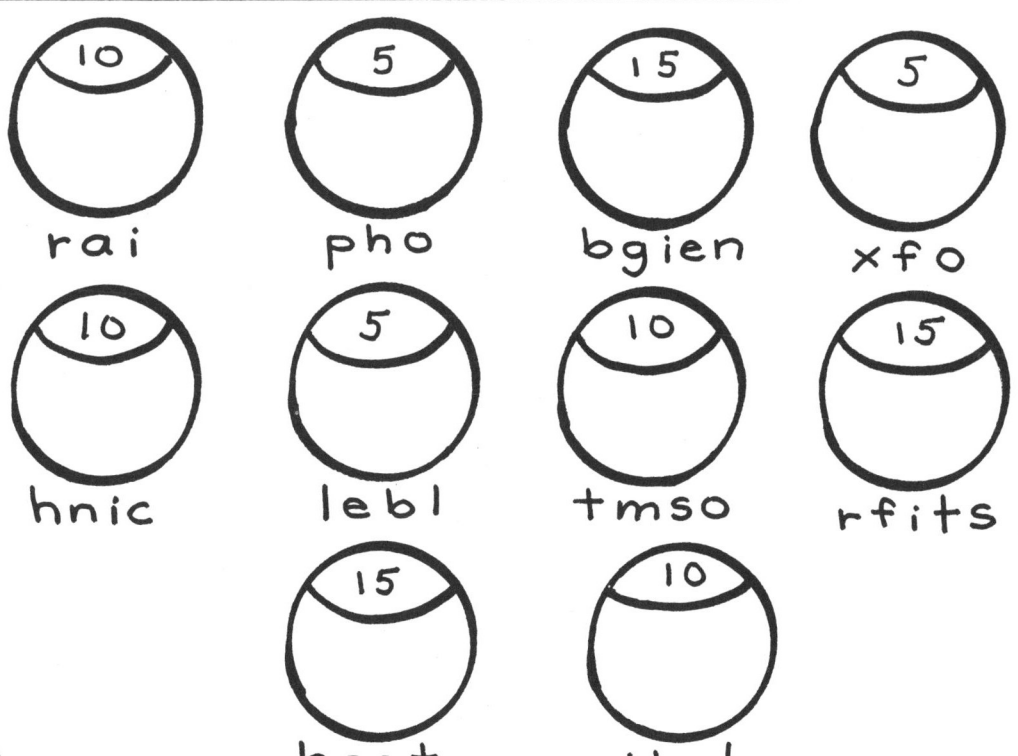

 100 points – 3 stars
90 points – 2 stars
75 points – 1 star

Score: _____

Directions: Arrange the letters in alphabetical order and write the word in the circle. Then add up your score to see how many stars you earned.

Name: _____

ALPHABETIZING

Directions: Write the following words in alphabetical order.

flower   apple   doll   ball   cat   egg

1. _____   4. _____
2. _____   5. _____
3. _____   6. _____

dish   fish   apron   box   eskimo   cap

1. _____   4. _____
2. _____   5. _____
3. _____   6. _____

Name: _____

ALPHABETIZING

Directions: Write the following words in alphabetical order.

1. _____   5. _____
2. _____   6. _____
3. _____   7. _____
4. _____   8. _____

1. _____   6. _____
2. _____   7. _____
3. _____   8. _____
4. _____   9. _____
5. _____   10. _____

Name: _____

ALPHABETIZING

Write the children's names in alphabetical order.

 Harry
 Jenifer
 Fred
 Olivia
 Bob
 Kathy
 Nan
 Ed
 Mary
 Carl
 Lil
 Dan
 Pat
 Inga

Boys

1. _____
2. _____
3. _____
4. _____
5. _____
6. _____
7. _____
8. _____

Girls

1. _____
2. _____
3. _____
4. _____
5. _____
6. _____
7. _____
8. _____

Gus

Alan

ALPHABETIZING

SHOPPING LIST

eggs
yams
ink
vegetables
tacos
lemons
squash
fruit
oranges
mints
Jello
Xerox
napkins
apples
pears
hash
bananas
carrots
umbrella
quilt
watermellon
zipper
radishes
donuts
grapes
Kleenex

Put the shopping list in alphabetical order.

A-D

E-H

I-L

M-P

Q-U

V-Z

Name: _____

ALPHABETIZING

The first letters of these words are different. Use the FIRST letter to alphabetize.

Number the words in alphabetical order.

	cat		put
	get		run
1	and		in
	have		kind
	boy		zoo
	end		that
	for		not
	did		want

Write the words in alphabetical order.

mother _____   queen _____
pretty _____   this   _____
on   _____   went   _____
if   _____   over   _____
kite   _____   read   _____
now   _____   you   _____
jump   _____   zebra _____
love   _____   under _____

Name:
ALPHABETIZING

The first letters of these words are the same.
Use the SECOND letter to alphabetize.

Number the words in alphabetical order.

☐	am
☐	ask
☐	art
☐	after
☐	and
☐	able
☐	add
☐	all

☐	send
☐	stop
☐	sing
☐	sun
☐	spoon
☐	soft
☐	say
☐	slide

Write the words in alphabetical order.

for _____
fly _____
father _____
full _____
fish _____
friend _____
fell _____

pen _____
pocket _____
plane _____
pick _____
prize _____
pull _____
past _____

Name: _____

ALPHABETIZING

The first two letters of these words are the same. Use the THIRD letter to alphabetize.

Number the words in alphabetical order.

☐ back	☐ peep
☐ ball	☐ pen
☐ baby	☐ pest
☐ bark	☐ pet
☐ band	☐ peach
☐ base	☐ pepper
☐ bat	☐ people
☐ bake	☐ peg

Write the words in alphabetical order.

rice _____   hope _____
ring _____   hot _____
right _____   hobby _____
rib _____   hold _____
ride _____   house _____
rip _____   horse _____
river _____   how _____
risk _____   home _____

Name:
ALPHABETIZING

The first three letters of these words are the same. Use the FOURTH letter to alphabetize.

Number the words in alphabetical order.

☐ flower	☐ cradle
☐ floral	☐ crayon
☐ floss	☐ crane
☐ float	☐ crate
☐ flood	☐ crack
☐ flock	☐ crawl
☐ flour	☐ crash
☐ flop	☐ crab

Write the words in alphabetical order.

place _____   spider _____
plaster _____   spies _____
play _____   spin _____
plate _____   spitz _____
plaza _____   spice _____
plain _____   spike _____
plan _____   spirit _____
plaque _____   spill _____

ALPHABETIZING

The first four letters of these words are the same. Use the FIFTH letter to alphabetize.

Number the words in alphabetical order.

☐ strength
☐ street
☐ stress
☐ strep
☐ stretch
☐ strew
☐ stream

☐ television
☐ telephone
☐ telecast
☐ telemeter
☐ telegram
☐ teletype
☐ telescope

Write the words in alphabetical order.

Complete _____   Workbook _____
compound _____   workman _____
compete _____   worker _____
compress _____   workable _____
company _____   workshop _____
compile _____   workout _____
compute _____   working _____

Name: _____

ALPHABETIZING

The first five letters of these words are the same. Use the SIXTH letter to alphabetize.

Number the words in alphabetical order.

- [ ] transfer
- [ ] transit
- [ ] transportation
- [ ] transcribe
- [ ] transmit
- [ ] transaction
- [ ] translate

- [ ] interest
- [ ] interfere
- [ ] interpret
- [ ] interupt
- [ ] interact
- [ ] interlock
- [ ] interview

Write the words in alphabetical order.

supermarket _____
superior _____
supervise _____
supersonic _____
superb _____
superlative _____
superhuman _____

crossing _____
crossroad _____
crosswalk _____
crossbar _____
crossover _____
crosspiece _____
crossed _____

179

ALPHABETIZING

Directions: Number the words in alphabetical order.

Use the <u>first</u> letter to alphabetize.

- success
- magazine
- experience
- agreement
- condition

Use the <u>second</u> letter to alphabetize.

- revolution
- royalty
- radiate
- rudiment
- rigorous

Use the <u>third</u> letter to alphabetize.

- preview
- praise
- principal
- prudence
- pronounce

Use the <u>fourth</u> letter to alphabetize.

- control
- conclude
- condition
- conference
- congratulate

Use the <u>fifth</u> letter to alphabetize.

- antique
- anticlimax
- antifreeze
- antidote
- antiseptic

Use the <u>sixth</u> letter to alphabetize.

- underneath
- underworld
- undertake
- underestimate
- understand

Name:

ALPHABETIZING

181
REVIEW

Directions: Alphabetize the following words.

climax _____
answer _____
handle _____
buffalo _____
territory _____
favorite _____
buckskin _____
feather _____

driftwood _____
starch _____
manuel _____
dramatize _____
provide _____
station _____
dredge _____
reserve _____

globe _____
children _____
gratitude _____
victory _____
electric _____
establish _____
childish _____
glory _____

construct _____
jewel _____
ultimate _____
written _____
constrain _____
library _____
young _____
ulterior _____

Name:
ALPHABETIZING REVIEW

Directions: Put a happy face ☺ over each column which is in alphabetical order and an unhappy face ☹ over each column which isn't in alphabetical order.

advance	contest	scramble	thirst
adventure	electric	screen	thought
advise	frequent	scratch	thread
advocate	justice	scrub	threshhold
affair	rotate	scribble	treasure
affect	trust	scroll	tweed
belong	sketch	concern	important
center	slide	concert	impossible
eagle	smooth	conclude	improve
defend	snail	condense	instant
formula	sweater	confident	interest
govern	swear	congress	invest
treasure	legible	supercharge	lessen
tremendous	necessary	supercool	lesson
tribute	pennant	superhuman	lesser
triangle	tenant	superfluous	letter
tricycle	vehicle	superman	level
triple	yearning	supersede	liberty

Name: _____

ENTRY WORDS

All the words listed in the dictionary are called "entry" words. These words are in **heavy** print and are listed in alphabetical order.

Directions: Open your dictionary to each page listed below and write the number of entry words you find on each page.

Page	Number of Entry Words	Page	Number of Entry Words
47	_____	98	_____
105	_____	15	_____
7	_____	137	_____
141	_____	166	_____
63	_____	54	_____
22	_____	195	_____
129	_____	71	_____
80	_____	39	_____

ENTRY WORDS

When looking for a word in the dictionary, always look for the **Root** of the word.
Ex. running - look for <u>run</u>.

<u>Directions</u>: Write the root word you would look for if you wanted to find the following words in the dictionary.

	Root Word		Root Word
1. coming	_____	9. biggest	_____
2. hoped	_____	10. cares	_____
3. friendly	_____	11. taken	_____
4. wanted	_____	12. stopping	_____
5. selves	_____	13. skater	_____
6. finest	_____	14. boxes	_____
7. hurries	_____	15. happily	_____
8. funnier	_____	16. tried	_____

Name: _____

DIVIDING THE DICTIONARY

It is easier to find an **entry** word if you divide the dictionary into three parts.

Write each of the following words under the section of the dictionary in which it can be found.

allow	garden	language	instant	protect	oppossum
tremble	value	balance	zero	surface	question
handsome	carriage	nonsense	explain	yonder	decide

| Front | Middle | End |
| A-G | H-P | Q-Z |

Name: _____

DIVIDING THE DICTIONARY

Directions: Put a check mark (✓) after each word in the column which indicates in which section of the dictionary it can be found.

	Front	Middle	End
	A-G	H-P	Q-Z
1. length			
2. usual			
3. baggage			
4. reply			
5. command			
6. jackdaw			
7. surround			
8. department			
9. otter			
10. whisper			
11. furniture			
12. mystery			

Name:

LOCATING ENTRY WORDS IN THE DICTIONARY

Now see how fast you can locate the following words in the dictionary. Write the page number and the column (1 or 2) where you found it. <u>Remember:</u> It helps to divide the dictionary into three sections.

	Page	Column		Page	Column
1. expect			9. imagine		
2. manage			10. realize		
3. journey			11. company		
4. astonish			12. quaint		
5. succeed			13. leather		
6. practice			14. umpire		
7. victory			15. target		
8. basement			16. direction		

GUIDE WORDS

To make it easier for you to find words in the dictionary, the **first** word and the **last** word on each page are printed on the top of each page. These are called "**Guide Words**."

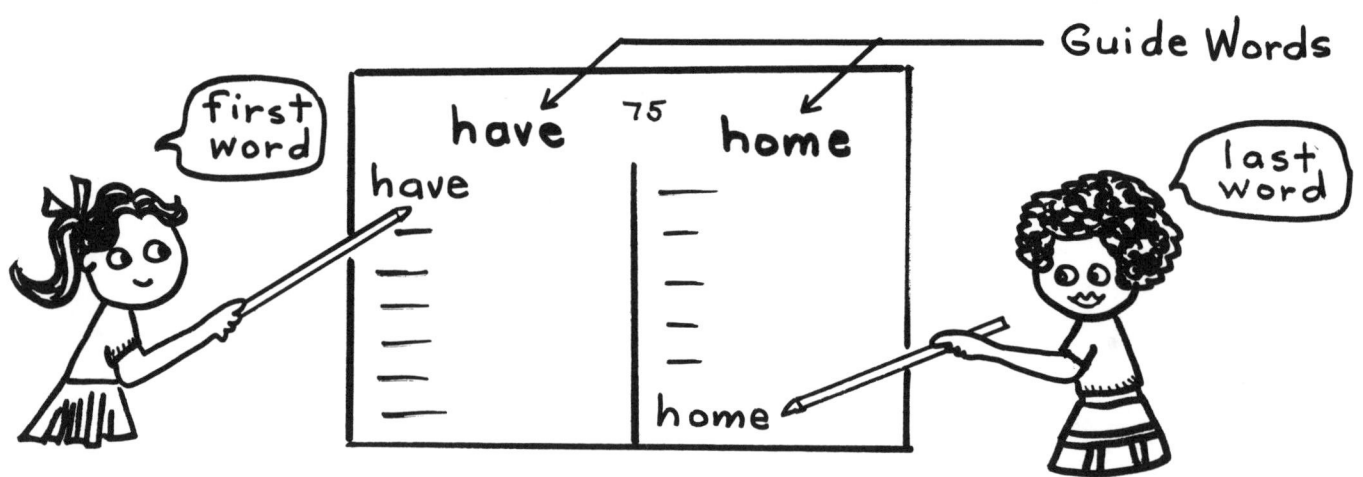

Directions: Find the Guide Words on the following pages of your dictionary. If the first entry word and the last entry word on the page are the same as the guide words, put a check mark (✓) in the Yes column. If they are not the same, put a check mark (✓) in the No column.

	Yes	No
page 17		
page 88		
page 36		
page 91		
page 64		

	Yes	No
page 102		
page 53		
page 9		
page 72		
page 48		

Name:
GUIDE WORDS

By looking at the guide words on each page, you will know which words are on that page - the words that come in alphabetical order between these words.

<u>Directions</u>: Write the guide words that you find on each of the following pages of your dictionary.

Page	Guide Words	Page	Guide Words
35	_____ _____	19	_____ _____
96	_____ _____	4	_____ _____
18	_____ _____	108	_____ _____
10	_____ _____	74	_____ _____
56	_____ _____	13	_____ _____
3	_____ _____	69	_____ _____
87	_____ _____	37	_____ _____
24	_____ _____	125	_____ _____

Name: _____

GUIDE WORDS

Directions: Find the following words in the dictionary. Write the number of the page on which you found it, the guide words on that page, and the entry word that comes before it and the entry word that comes after it.

	Page	Guide Words		Entry Word Before It	Entry Word After It
1. super			—		
2. fantastic			—		
3. great			—		
4. marvellous			—		
5. outstanding			—		
6. terrific			—		
7. wonderful			—		
8. excellent			—		
9. exceptional			—		
10. extraordinary			—		

Name:
GUIDE WORDS

Remember - Words that come in alphabetical order between the guide words will be on that page. Look at the guide words on each page below. Write the words that can be found on each page. Cross out the words that don't belong on any page.

ear	yarn	rust	rubber
yield	lamb	yet	cancel
land	right	late	large
rent	canal	lap	zero
candle	yolk	zeal	candy
result	lark	came	rock

111
camp   cane
_____
_____
_____
_____
_____

436
lamp   last
_____
_____
_____
_____
_____

947
yes   zebra
_____
_____
_____
_____
_____

681
rest   run
_____
_____
_____
_____
_____

Name:

GUIDE WORDS

Directions: Look at the guide words on each page below. Put a check mark (✓) next to the words that belong on the page and an "X" next to the words that don't belong on the page.

280

farm	few
__ farm	__ fellow
__ fair	__ fame
__ felt	__ fault
__ father	__ fan
__ fill	__ fence
__ fast	__ few

223

dish	door
__ dish	__ dove
__ display	__ ditto
__ doctor	__ double
__ dinner	__ divide
__ divine	__ dock
__ disappear	__ door

858

toy	try
__ toy	__ tribute
__ total	__ turn
__ trade	__ twice
__ treat	__ trust
__ toss	__ trace
__ transfer	__ try

451

light	look
__ light	__ loop
__ lime	__ log
__ long	__ lost
__ letter	__ line
__ lion	__ local
__ lick	__ look

Name: _____

GUIDE WORDS

Directions: Look at each set of guide words. If the word next to it would be on the same page, check "Yes." If not, check "No."

Guide Words	Word	Yes	No
1. hilltop - historic	hire		
2. plain - plant	plate		
3. secret - sedan	secretary		
4. cliff - clock	cloak		
5. acrobat - actuate	activity		
6. dither - division	document		
7. notebook - novelist	north		
8. seal - seat	search		
9. train - transfer	translate		
10. vision - vitrify	vitamin		
11. fame - far	farm		
12. quail - quarter	quality		
13. work - world	worn		
14. root - round	rough		
15. event - exact	exalt		

194

Name:
GUIDE WORDS

Directions: Look at the guide words below. Check whether the following words would be found **before** that page, **on** that page or **after** that page.

730

target   telephone

	Before	On	After
1. telescope			
2. temperature			
3. tabulate			
4. teaching			
5. tangible			
6. tapestry			
7. technical			
8. terrace			
9. tavern			
10. tenant			
11. telecast			
12. tactful			
13. tailor			
14. teller			
15. telegraph			

WORD DEFINITIONS

Next to each word in the dictionary is the meaning, or definition, of the word. Following are some words you probably don't know the meanings of. Find each word in the dictionary and write the meaning next to it.

1. quash

2. sachem

3. umbel

4. cadge

5. banyan

6. oboe

7. manse

8. cairn

Name:

WORD DEFINITIONS

Following are more words you probably don't know the meanings of. Find each word in the dictionary and write the meaning next to it.

1. jamb
2. waft
3. floe
4. dandle
5. lorry
6. talus
7. yawl
8. teak

WORD DEFINITIONS

Directions: Look up in the dictionary the meanings of the <u>underlined</u> words in the following questions. If the question gives the correct meaning, put a check mark (✓) in the "Yes" column. If the question doesn't give the correct meaning, put a check mark (✓) in the "No" column.

?	Yes	No
1. Is a <u>gauche</u> a bird?		
2. Is a <u>yegg</u> a sailboat?		
3. Is a <u>mahout</u> an elephant driver?		
4. Is a <u>davit</u> a large suitcase?		
5. Is a <u>gad</u> a sharp rod?		
6. Is a <u>daub</u> a smear or smudge?		
7. Is a <u>fane</u> a young princess?		
8. Is a <u>plebe</u> a wagon?		
9. Is a <u>zebu</u> an ox?		
10. Is a <u>scud</u> a wide driveway?		

Name: _____

WORD DEFINITIONS

Directions: When you look up some words in the dictionary, you may find words in the definition that you don't know the meanings of. In such a case, you will have to look up the meanings of those words too. Following are some words with their definitions. Look up the meaning of the underlined word in each definition and write a brief definition of it.

	Definition	Look up	Definition
admire	to have a high opinion of, <u>esteem</u>	esteem	
chide	to scold, <u>rebuke</u>	rebuke	
hinder	to get in the way, prevent, <u>impede</u>	impede	
gawk	to stare in <u>astonishment</u>	astonishment	
laud	to <u>extol</u>	extol	

Name: _____

WORD DEFINITIONS

Directions: When you look up some words in the dictionary, you may find words in the definition that you don't know the meanings of. In such a case, you will have to look up the meanings of those words too. Following are some words with their definitions. Look up the meaning of the underlined word in each definition and write a brief definition of it.

Definition	Look Up	Definition
venue — the place where the <u>alleged</u> events occurred	alleged	
special — <u>distinct</u> from all others	distinct	
mandatory — required by an official command, <u>compulsory</u>	compulsory	
plentiful — existing in great quantity, <u>abundant</u>	abundant	
liberal — favoring social progress, <u>tolerant</u>	tolerant	

Keep Looking

MULTIPLE MEANINGS

Many words in the dictionary have more than one meaning. The meaning of the word will depend on how it is used in the sentence. When more than one definition is given, each definition is numbered.

Ex. **bill** 1. statement of charges; 2. notice or poster; 3. draft of the law; 4. piece of paper money

Find each of the following words in the dictionary and write the number of meanings you find for each word.

Word	Number of Meanings	Word	Number of Meanings
leave	____	spread	____
wash	____	play	____
store	____	ram	____
lift	____	apply	____
post	____	blast	____
lock	____	sunrise	____
long	____	past	____
mind	____	reason	____

Name:
MULTIPLE MEANINGS

Find each of the following words in the dictionary and write the number of meanings you find for each word.

	Number of Meanings		Number of Meanings
cast	____	vent	____
umpire	____	ear	____
direction	____	outfit	____
beat	____	high	____
yellow	____	join	____
if	____	new	____
cold	____	tackle	____
face	____	zigzag	____
gain	____	quiet	____
table	____	kick	____

Name: _____

The dictionary will show you how to pronounce new words. Next to each entry word in the dictionary, there is a Phonic Respelling. Ex. said (sĕd). Note that in the Phonic Respelling you see only the letters you hear – no matter how the word may be spelled.

Most of the vowels in the respellings have special marks over them. Ex. (ă ē ŏ ä). These are called "Diacritical Marks". They will tell you what sound each vowel has in the respellings. Open your dictionary and look at some of the respellings next to the entry words. Don't try to read them yet.

THE PRONUNCIATION KEY

There is a Pronunciation key in the front of every dictionary, which tells you how to read the respellings. The Pronunciation key is needed because many symbols (letters) in our language have more than one sound. The Pronunciation key has just one (and only one) symbol for each sound in our language. Find the Pronunciation key in the front of your dictionary. Don't try to read it yet.

All dictionaries do not use the same Pronunciation key symbols. However, once you know how it works, you will be able to read the Pronunciation key in any dictionary.

Name: _____

THE PRONUNCIATION KEY

Now, let's find out how the Pronunciation Key works! Look at the Pronunciation Key below. You will note that there is a familiar word next to every symbol. These words are called "key Words." To find out what sound each symbol has, just look at the key Word next to it. The sound that each symbol has is the sound it will have in any respelling. Review every symbol in the Pronunciation Key below as follows:

Teacher: What sound does a have in the key Word at ?
Student: <u>a</u>te ?
Teacher: <u>c</u>are ?
" <u>a</u>
" <u>a</u>
" <u>a</u>
" etc.

Teacher: That's the sound a will have in any respelling.
" a
" ã
" ä
"
"

a - at	ē - we	ōō - too	ə
ā - ate	f - find	oi - oil	a - about
â - care	g - get	u - up	e - open
ä - father	h - he	ûr - fur	i - pencil
b - bed	i - in	p - pet	o - lemon
ch - child	ī - ice	r - red	u - circus
d - do	j - joy	s - see	
e - end	k - kite	sh - she	
	l - let	t - to	
	m - me	th - think	
	n - not	<u>th</u> - this	
	o - on	v - vase	
	ō - go	w - will	
	ô - order	y - you	
	ou - out	z - zoo	
	ŏŏ - look	zh - vision	

Name: _____

THE PRONUNCIATION KEY

Most dictionaries have a Shortened Pronunciation Key on the bottom of each right-hand page. The Shortened Pronunciation key lists the most difficult symbols. Check your dictionary to see if it has the Shortened Pronunciation Key on each right-hand page.

Now that you have some idea how the Pronunciation Key works, try to sound out the following respellings by using the Shortened Pronunciation key below, which has only long and short vowels. Remember: In the respelling, you see only the letters you hear — no matter how the word may be spelled.

1. (bāk) - What sound does ā have in the key word? - What's the word? __bake__
2. (hĕd) - What sound does ĕ have in the key word? - What's the word? _____
3. (slō) - What sound does ō have in the key word? - What's the word? _____
4. (hăv) - What sound does ă have in the key word? - What's the word? _____
5. (nīt) - What sound does ī have in the key word? - What's the word? _____
6. (wŭz) - What sound does ŭ have in the key word? - What's the word? _____
7. (nēt) - What sound does ē have in the key word? - What's the word? _____
8. (gŏn) - What sound does ŏ have in the key word? - What's the word? _____

ăt āte ĕnd wē ĭn īce ŏn gō ŭp ūse

See Answer Key

Name: _____

THE PRONUNCIATION KEY

MARK THE VOWEL
(Long + Short Vowels)

Directions: Put diacritical marks over the vowels in each row, which have the same sound as the first vowel. Be sure to check the pronunciation key below for any sounds you are not sure of.

ă	ăm	was	had	bake
ā	aim	take	car	said
ĕ	need	red	here	send
ē	be	ten	lead	her
ĭ	find	if	tie	win
ī	like	pie	give	big
ŏ	note	go	not	job
ō	hope	hop	coat	done
ŭ	full	cut	sun	cute
ū	mule	tune	put	fuel

ăt āte ĕnd wē ĭn īce ŏn·gō ŭp ūse

Note: Many dictionaries do not use diacritical marks over the short vowels in the respellings. Therefore, when you see an unmarked vowel, you know it is a short vowel. Ex. said (sed).

205

THE PRONUNCIATION KEY
(Long + Short Vowels)

Now see if it is easier to sound out the respellings, using just long and short vowels. Remember: In the respelling, you see only <u>the letters you hear</u> — no matter how the word may be spelled.

1. (hōp) — What sound does ō have in the key word? <u>hope</u> — What's the word? <u>hope</u>
2. (băt) — " " " ă " " " " ? ____ — " " " ? ____
3. (wĭl) — " " " ĭ " " " " ? ____ — " " " ? ____
4. (gĕt) — " " " ĕ " " " " ? ____ — " " " ? ____
5. (līk) — " " " ī " " " " ? ____ — " " " ? ____
6. (wăt) — " " " ă " " " " ? ____ — " " " ? ____
7. (hŏp) — " " " ŏ " " " " ? ____ — " " " ? ____
8. (sām) — " " " ā " " " " ? ____ — " " " ? ____
9. (sĕt) — " " " ĕ " " " " ? ____ — " " " ? ____
10. (fŭn) — " " " ŭ " " " " ? ____ — " " " ? ____

| ăt āte ĕnd wē ĭn īce ŏn gō ŭp ūse |

<u>Note</u>: In many one-syllable, short-vowel words the respelling is the same as the regular spelling because the word is already spelled phonetically. Ex. bat (băt).

Name: _____

THE PRONUNCIATION KEY
LET'S WRITE IT!

The best way to develop skill in pronouncing the respellings in the dictionary is to write some respellings yourself. Using the Pronunciation Key below, write the respelling for each of the following words.

Remember:
1. There is just one (and only <u>one</u>) symbol for each sound in the language.
2. In the respelling, you write <u>only the letters you hear</u>.

Short ă

1. man   (măn)
2. ran   ____
3. bag   ____
4. sat   ____
5. have ____
6. nap   ____
7. had   ____
8. bat   ____

Long ā

1. take   (tāk)
2. made   ____
3. way   ____
4. paid   ____
5. weigh ____
6. wait   ____
7. same   ____
8. tail   ____

ăt   āte

207

THE PRONUNCIATION KEY
LET'S WRITE IT!

Using the Pronunciation key below, write the respelling for each of the following words.

Remember:
1. There is just one (and only <u>one</u>) symbol for each sound in the language.
2. In the respelling, you write <u>only the letters you hear</u>.

Short ĕ

1. get — (gĕt)
2. pen — ____
3. bed — ____
4. hen — ____
5. said — ____
6. red — ____
7. head — ____
8. left — ____

Long ē

1. neat — (nēt)
2. seat — ____
3. be — ____
4. see — ____
5. team — ____
6. key — ____
7. real — ____
8. tea — ____

ĕnd   wē

Name: _____

THE PRONUNCIATION KEY
LET'S WRITE IT!

Now it's getting easy!

Using the Pronunciation key below, write the respelling for each of the following words.

Remember:
1. There is just one (and only <u>one</u>) symbol for each sound in the language.
2. In the respelling, you write <u>only the letters you hear</u>.

Short ĭ

1. will   (wĭl)
2. fill   _____
3. him   _____
4. big   _____
5. wish   _____
6. did   _____
7. give   _____
8. sit   _____

Long ī

1. night   (nīt)
2. right   _____
3. my   _____
4. like   _____
5. tie   _____
6. mile   _____
7. high   _____
8. ride   _____

| ĭn | īce |

THE PRONUNCIATION KEY
LET'S WRITE IT!

Using the Pronunciation key below, write the respelling for each of the following words.

Remember:
1. There is just one (and only <u>one</u>) symbol for each sound in the language.
2. In the respelling, you write <u>only the letters you hear</u>.

Short ŏ

1. hop   (hŏp)
2. job   _____
3. stop   _____
4. not   _____
5. rob   _____
6. lot   _____
7. mop   _____
8. got   _____

Long ō

1. show   (shō)
2. slow   _____
3. boat   _____
4. joke   _____
5. know   _____
6. soap   _____
7. toe   _____
8. no   _____

ŏn   gō

THE PRONUNCIATION KEY
LET'S WRITE IT!

Using the Pronunciation key below, write the respelling for each of the following words.

Remember:
1. There is just one (and only <u>one</u>) symbol for each sound in the language.
2. In the respelling, you write <u>only the letters you hear</u>.

Short ŭ

1. sun   (sŭn)
2. run   _____
3. dug   _____
4. shut _____
5. bus   _____
6. jump _____
7. won   _____
8. one   _____

Long ū = yōō

The sound of Long ū really represents two sounds — the consonant "y" and the vowel sound "ōō" as in the word "too." Therefore, it is always respelled "yōō" rather than "ū." See if you can respell the following words:

1. fuse   (fyōōz)
2. mule   _____
3. feud   _____
4. mute   _____
5. hue   _____
6. fume   _____
7. use   _____
8. few   _____

ŭp   ūse (yōō)

212

Name:

THE PRONUNCIATION KEY

Since the Pronunciation Key has one (and only <u>one</u>) symbol for each sound, <u>c</u> as in <u>cat</u> is respelled "k" and <u>c</u> as in <u>city</u> is respelled "s." Therefore, the symbol "c" doesn't appear in any respelling. Using the Pronunciation Key below, sound out each of the following respellings and write the word next to it:

c = k

1. (kăt)   cat
2. (kŭm)   ___
3. (băk)   ___
4. (kăn)   ___
5. (kyo͞ob) ___

c = s

1. (fās)   face
2. (rīs)   ___
3. (twīs) ___
4. (nīs)   ___
5. (rās)   ___

Since the Pronunciation Key has one (and only <u>one</u>) symbol for each sound, <u>g</u> as in <u>giraffe</u> is respelled "j." Using the Pronunciation Key below, sound out each of the following respellings and write the word next to it:

g = j

1. (āj)   age
2. (hyo͞oj) ___
3. (pāj)   ___
4. (jĕm)   ___
5. (wāj)   ___
6. (stāj) ___

| ăt āte ĕnd wē ĭn īce ŏn gō ŭp ūse (yo͞o) |

Name: _____

THE PRONUNCIATION KEY

Since the Pronunciation Key has one (and only one) symbol for each sound, x is respelled "ks." Therefore, the symbol "x" doesn't appear in any respelling. Using the Pronunciation Key below, sound out the following respellings and write the word next to it:

x = ks

1. (fĭks) _____
2. (mĭks) _____
3. (tăks) _____
4. (wăks) _____
5. (někst) _____

Since the Pronunciation Key has one (and only one) symbol for each sound, q is respelled "kw." Therefore, "q" doesn't appear in any respelling. Using the Pronunciation Key below, sound out the following respellings and write the word next to it:

q = kw

1. (kwĭk) _____
2. (kwăk) _____
3. (kwĭlt) _____
4. (kwĭz) _____
5. (kwĭt) _____
6. (kwāl) _____

ăt āte ĕnd wē ĭn īce ŏn gō ŭp ūse (yōō)

Name: _____

THE PRONUNCIATION KEY
(Long + Short Vowel Review)

Using the Pronunciation Key below, sound out the following respellings and write the word next to it:

1. (săt) _____
2. (lĭp) _____
3. (kŭm) _____
4. (pā) _____
5. (lĕt) _____
6. (pāj) _____
7. (rŭn) _____
8. (fĭks) _____

9. (fēl) _____
10. (jĕm) _____
11. (kīt) _____
12. (hōp) _____
13. (fās) _____
14. (kyo͞ob) _____
15. (tŏp) _____
16. (kwĕn) _____

ăt āte ĕnd wē ĭn īce ŏn gō ŭp ūse (yo͞o)

THE PRONUNCIATION KEY
MARK THE VOWEL
(Other Vowel Sounds)

Directions: Using the Pronunciation Key below, mark the vowel in each row which has the same sound as the first vowel.

ã	dãre	far	make	rare
ä	jar	late	card	tap
ô	hop	corn	lord	rope
o͝o	soon	book	pool	hook
o͞o	moon	cook	took	noon
û	curl	run	turn	tune

cãre fäther ôrder lo͝ok to͞o fûr

THE PRONUNCIATION KEY
LET'S WRITE IT!

Using the Pronunciation key below, write the respelling for each of the following words.

Remember:
1. There is just one (and only <u>one</u>) symbol for each sound in the language.
2. In the respelling, you write <u>only</u> <u>the</u> <u>letters</u> <u>you</u> <u>hear</u>.

ã

1. dare (dãr)
2. fare ____
3. share ____
4. bare ____
5. hare ____
6. pear ____

ä

1. jar (jär)
2. far ____
3. part ____
4. star ____
5. car ____
6. large ____

cãre   fäther

Name: _____

THE PRONUNCIATION KEY
LET'S WRITE IT!

Using the Pronunciation key below, write the respelling for each of the following words:

ô   o͝o   o͞o

1. lord (lôrd)   1. could (ko͝od)   1. fruit (fro͞ot)

2. born _____   2. would _____   2. moon _____

3. worn _____   3. book _____   3. tune _____

4. form _____   4. put _____   4. new _____

5. warm _____   5. full _____   5. blue _____

```
order      look      too
```

Name: _____

THE PRONUNCIATION KEY
LET'S WRITE IT!

Using the Pronunciation Key below, write the respelling for each of the following words:

Remember:
1. There is just one (and only <u>one</u>) symbol for each sound in the language.
2. In the respelling, you write <u>only the letters you hear</u>.

û

1. curl (kûrl)
2. turn _____
3. surf _____
4. burn _____
5. furl _____
6. surge _____

Since the Pronunciation Key has one (and only one) symbol for each sound, <u>er</u> and <u>ir</u> are respelled "ûr." Sound out the respellings below and write the word next to it:

er = ûr

1. her (hûr)
2. fern _____
3. herd _____
4. germ _____

ir = ûr

1. fir _____
2. bird _____
3. girl _____
4. first _____

fûr

THE PRONUNCIATION KEY

Since the Pronunciation Key has one (and only one) symbol for each sound, ow is respelled "ou" and oy is respelled "oi." Sound out the respellings below and write the word next to it.

oi
1. (boi) boy
2. (toi) ____
3. (joi) ____
4. (koi) ____
5. (soi) ____

ou
1. (hou) how
2. (nou) ____
3. (kou) ____
4. (wou) ____
5. (doun) ____

LET'S WRITE IT!

Using the Pronunciation Key below, write the respelling for each of the following words:

oy = oi
1. toy ( )
2. ploy ____
3. boy ____
4. cloy ____
5. joy ____

ow = ou
1. cow ____
2. frown ____
3. plow ____
4. vow ____
5. brown ____

oil   out

THE PRONUNCIATION KEY

Using the Pronunciation Key below, sound out the following respellings and write the word next to it:

th

1. (thĭn) ____
2. (thĭk) ____
3. (thrē) ____
4. (wĭth) ____

th̸

1. (th̸ăt) ____
2. (th̸ēz) ____
3. (th̸ōz) ____
4. (th̸ĕm) ____

LET'S WRITE IT!

Using the Pronunciation Key below, write the respelling for each of the following words:

th or th̸ ?

1. teeth ____
2. than ____
3. thumb ____
4. they ____
5. third ____
6. fifth ____
7. then ____
8. thump ____

| think | th̸is |

Name: _____

THE PRONUNCIATION KEY

Following is a review of all the Pronunciation Key symbols we have covered so far. Using the Pronunciation Key below, sound out each respelling and write the word next to it:

1. (frē) _____
2. (no͞o) _____
3. (nīf) _____
4. (bāk) _____
5. (hĭz) _____
6. (swôrn) _____
7. (dŭk) _____
8. (thĭn) _____

9. (kwĭt) _____
10. (plās) _____
11. (nou) _____
12. (lärj) _____
13. (sho͝od) _____
14. (gŏt) _____
15. (hûr) _____
16. (thĕm) _____

17. (blō) _____
18. (ko͝ok) _____
19. (brĕd) _____
20. (fĭks) _____
21. (dâr) _____
22. (toi) _____
23. (fyo͞o) _____
24. (lûrn) _____

ăt āte câre fäther ĕnd ēwe ĭn īce ŏn gō
ôrder lo͝ok to͞o oil ŭp fûr think *this*

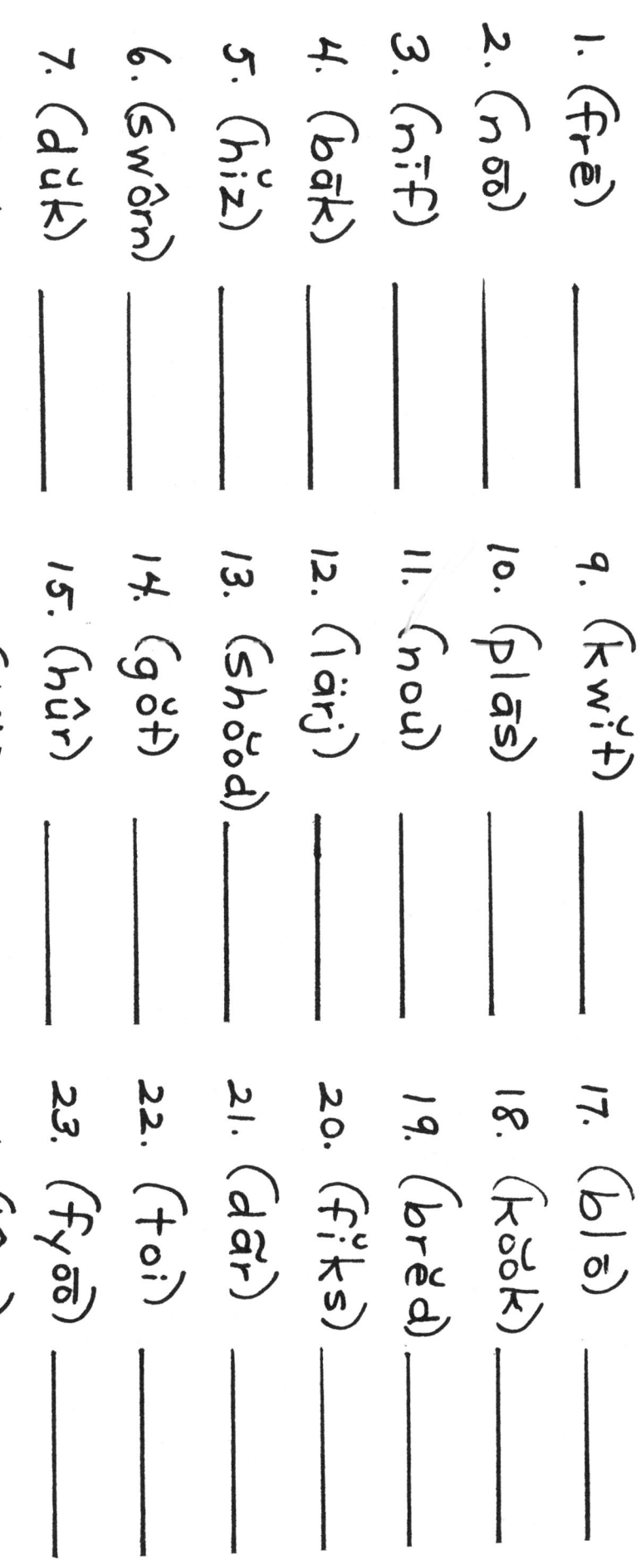

Read the following riddles and translate the answers into regular spelling.

Joe: Why is it always cool in the baseball stadium?
Ted: (bē kŭz´) (thĕr) (ĭz) (ā) (făn) (ĭn) (ĕv´rē) (sēt)

Joe: What did one strawberry say to the other strawberry?
Ted: (ĭf) (yoo) (wûrn't) (sō) (frĕsh) (wē) (woodn't) (bē) (ĭn) (this) (jăm)

Joe: Why does a cow need a bell?
Ted: (bē kŭz´) (hĭz) (hôrnz) (dōn't) (wûrk)

Joe: What did one elevator say to the other elevator?
Ted: (ī) (thĭnk) (ī) (ăm) (kŭm´ĭng) (doun) (wĭth) (sŭm´thĭng)

Joe: How long will an eight-day clock run without winding?
Ted: (ĭt) (wōn't) (rŭn) (āt) (ôl) (wĭth out´) (wīnd´ĭng)

Joe: What is the best way to catch a squirrel?
Ted: (klīm) (ā) (trē) (ănd) (ăkt) (līk) (ā) (nŭt)

THE PRONUNCIATION KEY

Yikes! Is this English?

Here are some words you probably don't know. Now, you'll see how the Pronunciation Key will show you how to pronounce new words. See if you can sound out the respellings below, using the Pronunciation Key below. What sound does the symbol have in the key word? That is the sound it will have in the respelling.

1. chic (shēk)
2. gauge (gāj)
3. reign (rān)
4. heist (hīst)
5. toque (tōk)
6. gnome (nōm)
7. ache (āk)
8. blase (blä zā')
9. plaque (plăk)
10. niche (nĭch)
11. gnu (no͞o)
12. gauche (gōsh)
13. ewe (yo͞o)
14. cache (kăsh)
15. gneiss (nīs)
16. palm (päm)

ăt āte câre fäther ĕnd wē ĭn īce ŏn gō ôrder lo͝ok to͞o out oil ŭp fûr think ~~this~~

THE PRONUNCIATION KEY
The Schwa - ə

When a vowel is in the <u>unaccented</u> syllable, it does not have its true, full sound. You can hardly hear it. Ex. <u>a</u>'bout, moth'<u>e</u>r, pen'c<u>i</u>l, lem'<u>o</u>n, cir'c<u>u</u>s. This sound of the vowels is represented by the symbol "ə," which is called a "schwa." It looks like an upside-down e. The sound of this symbol is much like the sound of short u, or "uh." Using the Pronunciation Key below, sound out each of the following respellings and write the word next to it:

1. (ə wā')   away
2. (kĭch'ən) _____
3. (rŏb'ən) _____
4. (wăg'ən) _____
5. (mī'nəs) _____

6. (ə grē') _____
7. (ŭn'dər) _____
8. (stĕn'səl) _____
9. (pī'lət) _____
10. (bō'nəs) _____

ə for a, e, i, o, u in about, open, pencil, lemon, circus

Name: _____ 225

THE PRONUNCIATION KEY
The Schwa - ə

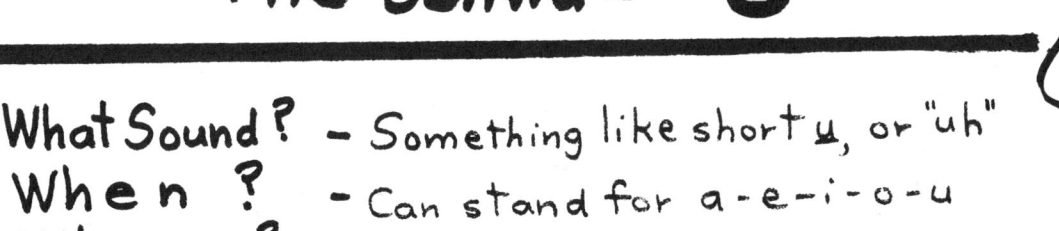

What Sound? — Something like short u, or "uh"
When? — Can stand for a-e-i-o-u
Where? — On the unaccented syllable
Why? — Because you can hardly hear it

Sound out each respelling below and write the word next to it.

1. (ā′prəl) _____   6. (kăk′təs) _____
2. (nĭk′əl) _____   7. (kăb′ən) _____
3. (roi′əl) _____   8. (rā′zər) _____
4. (hōp′fəl) _____   9. (ə sīd′) _____
5. (bŏt′əm) _____   10. (pŏk′ət) _____

ə for a, e, i, o, u in about, open, pencil, lemon, circus

THE PRONUNCIATION KEY
The Schwa- ə

What Sound? — Something like short u, or "uh"
When? — Can stand for a-e-i-o-u
Where? — On the unaccented syllable
Why? — Because you can hardly hear it

<u>le</u> is usually respelled "əl." Sound out the following respellings and write the word next to it.

1. (hăn′dəl) _____
2. (sĭm′pəl) _____
3. (no͞o′dəl) _____
4. (skrăm′bəl) _____
5. (ē′gəl) _____
6. (jŭg′əl) _____
7. (tĕm′pəl) _____
8. (pûr′pəl) _____
9. (stē′pəl) _____
10. (kăn′dəl) _____

ə for a, e, i, o, u in <u>a</u>bout, op<u>e</u>n, penc<u>i</u>l, lem<u>o</u>n, circ<u>u</u>s

Name: _____ 227

PRONUNCIATION KEY

Draw the Picture
Write the Word

Using the Pronunciation Key below, sound out each respelling, draw the picture, and write the regular spelling below the picture.

(kŭp)	(shûrt)	(ô′tō mə bēl)	(kwēn)
(kloun)	(kīt)	(wăg′ən)	(bûrth′dā) (kāk)
(froot)	(brĭj)	(härn)	(tûr′kē)

ăt āte cãre fäther ĕnd wē ĭn īce ŏn gō ôrder look too out
oil ŭp fûr think this   ə = a-about, e-open, i-pencil, o-lemon, u-circus

Name:
THE PRONUNCIATION KEY
zh

There is a sound in the English language that does not have a symbol to represent it. It is the sound like s in the word "vision." This sound is represented in the respelling by the symbol "zh." Sound out the respellings below and write the word next to it:

1. (lē′zhər) __leisure__

2. (trĕzh′ər) _____

3. (vĭzh′ən) _____

4. (mĕzh′ər) _____

5. (yōō′zhōō əl) _____

6. (rĭ vĭzh′ən) _____

7. (plĕzh′ər) _____

8. (dĭ vĭzh′ən) _____

```
zh - vision
```

Name: _____

THE PRONUNCIATION KEY
LET'S WRITE IT!

Using the Pronunciation Key below, write the respelling for each of the following words.

Remember:
1. There is just one (and only <u>one</u>) symbol for each sound in the language.
2. In the respelling, you write <u>only the letters you hear</u>.

ə

1. alone   (ə lōn′)
2. after   _____
3. bonus   _____
4. cabin   _____
5. dragon _____
6. canoe   _____
7. number _____
8. minus   _____

zh

1. division (di vizh′ən)
2. pleasure _____
3. measure   _____
4. treasure _____

---
zh - vi<u>s</u>ion   ə - a-about, e-open, i-pencil, o-lemon, u-circus
---

230

THE PRONUNCIATION KEY

Following is a complete review of all the Pronunciation key symbols we have covered. Using the Pronunciation Key below, sound out each respelling and write the word next to it:

1. (ho͞o) _____
2. (mĭks) _____
3. (ə wā´) _____
4. (fĭl) _____
5. (drĕs) _____
6. (sho͝o) _____
7. (bôrn) _____
8. (the) _____

9. (thûrd) _____
10. (po͞ol) _____
11. (twīs) _____
12. (shâr) _____
13. (härt) _____
14. (kyo͞ot) _____
15. (boi) _____
16. (kwăk) _____

17. (plā) _____
18. (mĕzh´ər) _____
19. (ko͝od) _____
20. (jə răf´) _____
21. (gĭv) _____
22. (lĕm´ən) _____
23. (no͞ok) _____
24. (kloun) _____

ă-at āte câre fäther ĕnd wē ĭn īce ŏn gō ôrder lo͝ok to͞o out oil ŭp fûr think this zh-vision ə=a-about, e-open, i-pencil, o-lemon, u-circus

Read the following riddles and translate the answers into regular spelling.

Joe: Why didn't the chicken cross the street?
Ted: (bē kŭz´) (hē) (wŭz) (chĭk´ən)

Joe: Why did the turtle cross the street?
Ted: (bē kŭz´) (thĕr) (wŭz) (ə) (shĕl) (stā´shən) (ŏn) (thə) (ŭth´ər) (sīd)

Joe: How do you get down from an elephant?
Ted: (yōō) (dōn't) - (yōō) (gĕt) (doun) (frŭm) (ə) (gōōs)

Joe: What is the difference between a big hill and a big pill?
Ted: (wŭn) (ĭz) (härd) (tōō) (gĕt) (ŭp) (thə) (ŭth´ər) (ĭz) (härd) (tōō) (gĕt) (doun)

Joe: How many monkeys can you put into an empty barrel?
Ted: (wŭn) - (ăf´tər) (thăt) (thə) (băr´əl) (ĭz´n't) (ĕmp´tē)

Joe: What do you get when you cross a parrot with a tiger?
Ted: (thā) (dōn't) (nō) (bŭt) (hwĕn) (ĭt) (tŏks) (ĕv´rē bŏd ē) (lĭs´ənz)

Name: _____

PRONUNCIATION KEY REVIEW

Now that you have acquired some expertise in reading respellings, let's see how quickly you can transcribe these super-tough words.

1. (kəm plēt′) _____

2. (di sizh′ən) _____

3. (in′tər əst) _____

4. (di lish′əs) _____

5. (sit′ē) _____

6. (fôr mā′shən) _____

7. (kən fyoō′zhən) _____

8. (bī′si kəl) _____

9. (jen′ər əl) _____

10. (kwol′ə tē) _____

11. (pär′ti kəl) _____

12. (dif′ər ənt) _____

13. (pou′ər fəl) _____

14. (en joi′ə bəl) _____

15. (i loō′mə nāt) _____

16. (ə grē′ə bəl) _____

ăt āte câre fäther ĕnd wē ĭn īce ŏn gō ôrder loŏk toō out oil ŭp fûr think this zh-vision ə-a-about, e-open, i-pencil, o-lemon, u-circus

Name: _____ 233

DICTIONARY SKILLS
For Experts Only

Remember: All dictionaries do not have the same Pronunciation Key symbols. Using the Pronunciation key below, respell, syllabify, and accent the following words. Then check out each answer in your dictionary.

	Respell, Syllabify, and Accent	Check the Word in Your Own Dictionary		
		Page	Right	Wrong	Same	Different
1. over	(ō′ vər)		✓			
2. moon						
3. bird						
4. corner						
5. fuel						
6. share						
7. could						
8. vision						

ă at ā ate â care ä father ĕ end ē we ĭ in ī ice ŏ on ō go ô order o͝o look o͞o too ou out oi oil u up û fûr th think <u>th</u> this zh-vision ə = a-about, e-open, i-pencil, o-lemon, u-circus

ANSWER KEY

p. 204
1. bake
2. head
3. slow
4. have
5. night
6. was
7. heat
8. gone

p. 205

ă	ăm	hăd
ā	āim	tāke
ĕ	rĕd	sĕnd
ē	bē	lēad
ĭ	ĭf	wĭn
ī	līke	pīe
ŏ	nŏt	jŏb
ō	hōpe	cōat
ŭ	cŭt	sŭn
ū	mūle	fūel

p. 206
1. hope
2. bat
3. will
4. get
5. like
6. wait
7. hope
8. same
9. seat
10. fun

p. 207
1. (măn)
2. (răn)
3. (băg)
4. (săt)
5. (hăv)
6. (năp)
7. (hăd)
8. (băt)

1. (tāk)
2. (mād)
3. (wā)
4. (pād)
5. (wā)
6. (wāt)
7. (sām)
8. (tāl)

p. 208
1. (gĕt)
2. (pĕn)
3. (bĕd)
4. (hĕn)
5. (sĕd)
6. (rĕd)
7. (hĕd)
8. (lĕft)

1. (hēt)
2. (sēt)
3. (bē)
4. (sē)
5. (tēm)
6. (kē)
7. (rēl)
8. (tē)

p. 209
1. (wĭl)
2. (fĭl)
3. (hĭm)
4. (bĭg)
5. (wĭsh)
6. (dĭd)
7. (gĭv)
8. (sĭt)

1. (hīt)
2. (rīt)
3. (mī)
4. (līk)
5. (tī)
6. (mī)
7. (hī)
8. (rīd)

ANSWER KEY

p. 210
1. (hŏp)
2. (jŏb)
3. (stŏp)
4. (nŏt)
5. (rŏb)
6. (lŏt)
7. (mŏp)
8. (gŏt)
5. (shō)
6. (slō)
3. (bōt)
4. (jōk)
5. (nō)
6. (sōp)
7. (tō)
8. (nō)

p. 211
1. (sŭn)
2. (rŭn)
3. (dŭg)
4. (shŭt)
5. (bŭs)
6. (jŭmp)
7. (wŭn)
8. (wŭn)
1. (fyōoz)
2. (myōol)
3. (fyōod)
4. (myōot)
5. (hyōo)
6. (fyōom)
7. (yōoz)
8. (fyōo)

p. 212
1. cat
2. come
3. back
4. can
5. cube
1. face
2. rice
3. twice
4. nice
5. race
1. age
2. huge
3. page
4. gem
5. wage
6. stage

p. 213
1. fix
2. mix
3. tax
4. wax
5. next
1. quick
2. quack
3. quit
4. quiz
5. quit
6. quail

p. 214
1. sat
2. lip
3. come
4. pay
5. let
6. page
7. run
8. fix
9. feel
10. gem
11. kite
12. hope
13. face
14. cube
15. top
16. queen

p. 215
ā — dãre rãre
ä : — jär cärd
ô ⟨o⟩ — côrn lôrd
ŏŏ — bŏŏk hŏŏk
ōō — mōon nōon
û — cârl tûrn

ANSWER KEY

P. 216
1. (där)
2. (fär)
3. (shär)
4. (bär)
5. (här)
6. (pär)

1. (jär)
2. (fär)
3. (pärt)
4. (stär)
5. (kär)
6. (lärj)

P. 217
1. (lôrd) 1. (kôrd) 1. (froot)
2. (bôrn) 2. (wood) 2. (moon)
3. (wôrn) 3. (book) 3. (toon)
4. (fôrm) 4. (poot) 4. (noo)
5. (wôrm) 5. (toot) 5. (bloo)

P. 218
1. (kûrl) 1. (bûrn)
2. (tûrn) 2. (fûrl)
3. (sûrf) 3. (sûrj)

1. (hûr) 1. (fûr)
2. (fûrm) 2. (bûrd)
3. (hûrd) 3. (gûrl)
4. (jûrm) 4. (fûrst)

P. 219
1. boy
2. toy
3. joy
4. coy
5. soy

1. how
2. now
3. cow
4. wow
5. down

1. (toi)   1. (kou)
2. (ploi)   2. (froun)
3. (boi)   3. (plou)
4. (kloi)   4. (vou)
5. (joi)   5. (broun)

P. 220
1. thin   1. that
2. thick   2. these
3. three   3. those
4. with   4. them

1. (tēth)   5. (thûrd)
2. (thăn)   6. (fĭfth)
3. (thŭm)   7. (thĕn)
4. (thā)   8. (thŭmp)

P. 221
1. free   9. quit   17. blow
2. new   10. place   18. cook
3. knife 11. now   19. bread
4. bake   12. large   20. fix
5. his   13. should 21. dare
6. sworn 14. got   22. toy
7. duck   15. her   23. few
8. thin   16. them   24. learn

ANSWER KEY

p. 224
1. away 6. agree
2. kitchen 7. under
3. robin 8. stencil
4. wagon 9. pilot
5. minus 10. bonus

p. 225
1. April 6. cactus
2. nickel 7. cabin
3. royal 8. razor
4. hopeful 9. aside
5. bottom 10. pocket

p. 226
1. handle 6. juggle
2. simple 7. temple
3. noodle 8. purple
4. scramble 9. steeple
5. eagle 10. candle

p. 228
1. leisure 5. usual
2. treasure 6. revision
3. vision 7. pleasure
4. measure 8. division

p. 229
1. (ə lōn′) 5. (drăg′ən)
2. (ăf′tər) 6. (kə no͞o′)
3. (bō năs) 7. (nŭm′bər)
4. (kă′bən) 8. (mī′nəs)

1. (dĭ vĭzh′ən) 3. (mĕzh′ər)
2. (plĕzh′ər) 4. (trĕzh′ər)

p. 230
1. who 9. third 17. play
2. mix 10. pull 18. measure
3. away 11. twice 19. could
4. fill 12. share 20. giraffe
5. dress 13. heart 21. give
6. shoe 14. cute 22. lemon
7. born 15. boy 23. knock
8. the 16. quack 24. clown

Answer Key

p. 232

1. complete	9. general
2. decision	10. quality
3. interest	11. particle
4. delicious	12. different
5. city	13. powerful
6. formation	14. enjoyable
7. confusion	15. illuminate
8. bicycle	16. agreeable

p. 233

Check this one out yourself in the dictionary!

The End